THE
LITTLE
BOOK
OF
IRISH
LANDMARKS

CATHAL COYLE

The
History
Press
Ireland

*To my father Aidan, who introduced me to many of the landmarks
mentioned in this book during my childhood*

First published 2017

The History Press Ireland
50 City Quay
Dublin 2
Ireland
www.thehistorypress.ie

The History Press Ireland is a member of Publishing Ireland,
the Irish Book Publishers' Association.

© Cathal Coyle, 2017

British Library Cataloguing in Publication Data.
A catalogue record for this book is available from the British Library.

ISBN 978 1 84588 226 6

Typesetting and origination by The History Press
Printed and bound by TJ International Ltd

CONTENTS

ACKNOWLEDGEMENTS

I would like to thank my family: Louise, Caoimhe, Dáire and Ruairí for their help and support during the research and writing of this book and I would like to dedicate this book to them. Thanks to Adam Kee for his illustrations, and to Beth Amphlett and Ronan Colgan from The History Press for giving me the opportunity to write this book – and for all their assistance throughout.

GLOSSARY

Bawn a fortified walled enclosure, part of a tower-house or medieval castle

Bronze Age approximately between 2400 BC and 500 BC; between the Stone Age and Iron Age

Cairn a mound of stones

Capstone a massive stone, weighing as much as 100 tonnes, covering a megalithic tomb

Cashel a stone-built circular enclosure

Celt Iron Age culture arriving in Ireland around 300 BC

Chevaux-de-frise projecting sharp stones placed in the ground outside an Iron Age Fort to deter an enemy

Corbel a stone projecting from a wall face, designed to support a widening of the wall or a wooden beam

Court-tomb earliest kind of megalithic burial site

Crannòg ancient lake dwelling

Dolmen megalithic tomb consisting of a flat stone laid on upright ones

Gaeltacht an Irish-speaking district

Hillfort enclosed sites, usually of several hectares/acres, consisting of one or more banks and ditches surrounding a hilltop, often following the contours of the land

Iron Age from circa 500 BC to the arrival of Christianity; the period most associated with Ireland's 'Royal' sites such as Tara and Rathcroghan

Keep the central tower of a castle

Martello Tower tower built on coasts for protection against an expected Napoleonic invasion by sea

Megalithic 'big stone' a term that refers to the many different types of large prehistoric stone tombs

Neolithic late Stone Age, 4000 BC–2000 BC

Ogham an Irish script from the early centuries AD inscribed on standing stones

Passage Grave a megalithic tomb consisting of a corridor of stones leading to a burial chamber

Penal Laws a series of repressive laws that originated in the seventeenth century, and were imposed on Roman Catholics and Protestant dissenters

Ráth (or ringfort) ancient dwelling place surrounded by a rampart

Ringfort these are known by a variety of names, including fort, *ráth, dún, lios, cashel* and *caher*. They consist of an area, usually circular, enclosed by one or more earthen banks or, occasionally, by stone walls

Romanesque a style of architecture using the Roman or semi-circular arch, which was a favoured style in Ireland during the twelfth century

Society of United Irishmen a revolutionary republican organisation that launched the 1798 Rising in Ireland with the objective of ending British monarchical rule over Ireland and founding an independent Irish Republic

Stone Circle a ring of standing stones, usually freestanding, enclosing an open area, sometimes with a grave or burial mound at the centre

The Ulster Cycle one of the four great cycles of Irish mythology, is a body of medieval Irish heroic legends and sagas of the traditional heroes of the Ulaid in what is now eastern Ulster and northern Leinster

Wedge Tomb the most numerous of Ireland's megalithic tombs, usually date to the Late Neolithic or Early Bronze Age periods

* * * *

Irish words associated with landmarks

In visiting many of the landmarks that are outlined in this book, you will find that many Irish words remain an intrinsic part of site names and towns, etc. Here are some of the most common such words:

Abhainn (owen) river
Ard/Art height
Áth ford
Baile town
Beag (beg) small
Carraig (carrick) rock

Cill (kill) church or monk's cell
Cloch stone
Cnoc (knock) hill
Dearg (derg) red
Droichead bridge
Droim (drum) back or ridge of a hill
Dubh black
Dún a fort
Inis (Inish) island
Lios (lis) fort (also Dún)
Mágh plain
Mór (more) large
Mullach (mullagh) peak
Ráth ringfort
Sliabh (slieve) mountain
Teach (ti, tigh) church, house
Teampall (temple) church
Trá strand
Tulach hill, hillock

INTRODUCTION

The term 'landmark' can conjure up many subjective definitions when thinking about Ireland. Should it be confined to geographical features such as Croagh Patrick or the River Shannon? Or should it factor in city buildings such as the Mansion House in Dublin?

This book strives to be as inclusive as possible, featuring an array of landmarks: from rivers, hills, mountains and loughs to historic monuments and the built environment such as Drombeg Stone Circles in County Cork and the Guildhall in Derry. It features the 'old' – or ancient – and the 'new' – or modern.

Ancient sites proliferate throughout Ireland, including the world's oldest Stone Age monuments at the Céide Fields in County Mayo. Early Christian churches, round towers and charismatic castles reflect a diverse history over thousands of years.

Mythology is closely associated with many ancient landmarks in Ireland – the Giant's Causeway and Fionn Mac Cumhaill is one of the most famous, and I have endeavoured to mention stories and legends attached to some of these landmarks.

The landmarks mentioned are just some examples of those that are visited by thousands of people each year. The warm *Céad Míle Fáilte* (a hundred thousand welcomes) that is offered to guests indeed speaks volumes, contributing to the island's reputation as 'Ireland of the Welcomes'.

And it is not just Irish people who visit these landmarks. Irish tourism from overseas has enjoyed a resurgence in recent years. According to Tourism Ireland, there was a 17 per cent growth in visitors from outside Ireland for the first quarter of 2016. This translates into an increased number of people across the globe having the opportunity to view our many wonderful Irish landmarks.

This book celebrates the diversity of Ireland – from the Wild Atlantic Way and its rugged natural wonders such as the Cliffs of Moher, to the urban centres that contain landmark buildings such as Trinity College in Dublin, as well as city icons such as the 'Samson and Goliath' cranes in Belfast.

This book details a selection of these Irish landmarks – from the natural (the Dark Hedges) to the ancient (Newgrange) to the recent (Dublin's iconic Spire on O'Connell Street, thought to be the tallest sculpture in the world).

While many of the landmarks mentioned in this book belong to a specific county, such as Slemish Mountain in County Antrim, there are certain landmarks such as rivers that flow through several counties – and in some cases different provinces.

I have referred to the subjective nature of this selection and, admittedly, there are landmarks selected that are nostalgic to me as a result of my own experiences. But I hope I have selected a broad and diverse range that gives you the reader a flavour of the many inspiring landmarks that are found throughout the island of Ireland.

For anyone who has the pleasure of visiting any of these Irish landmarks, I offer this traditional Irish blessing of goodwill on your journey:

May the road rise to meet you,
May the wind be always at your back,
The sunshine warm upon your face,
The rainfall soft upon your fields.

IRISH PROVINCES

The Old Irish word for province, *cóiced*, (now *cúige*) also means a fifth. Some scholars believe that as well as the current four provinces – Connacht (west); Leinster (east); Munster (south); Ulster (north), there was also a mystical fifth province – *Mide*. It was thought to be the central province around which the others formed. In terms of place, it is thought to be the Hill of Uisneach, now in County Westmeath (see Chapter 2).

The current Irish provinces include the thirty-two counties of Ireland that are referred to during the course of this book:

Connacht
The western province, Connacht, is bounded by the River Shannon in the east and the Atlantic Ocean in the west. There are many

outstanding geographical landmarks in Connacht, such as Croagh Patrick, a mountain in County Mayo, and Lough Corrib. Connacht has five counties:

Galway	Mayo	Sligo
Leitrim	Roscommon	

Leinster

The south-east province, it also includes the mythical fifth province of *Mide*. It is here that the Hill of Uisneach, the symbolic centre of Ireland, is found. This spiritual heritage can also be found at sites such as Knowth and Tara in County Meath. The capital city of Dublin contains landmarks such as the 'Ha'Penny Bridge'. Leinster has twelve counties:

Carlow	Laois	Offaly
Dublin	Longford	Westmeath
Kildare	Louth	Wexford
Kilkenny	Meath	Wicklow

Munster

The south-west province, with coastal landmarks such as the Cliffs of Moher in County Clare and islands such as Valentia in County Kerry, can be breathtaking. Man-made structures such as Blarney Castle in County Cork and the numerous stone circles such as Drombeg prove the diversity of this province's many landmarks. The six counties of Munster are:

Clare	Kerry	Tipperary
Cork	Limerick	Waterford

Ulster

The northern province, with nine counties. It is a province of stone circles and dolmens, and the largest lake in Ireland, Lough Neagh – with five of Ulster's counties touching its shores. Ulster is closely associated with Ireland's patron saint, Patrick, who spent time in his youth at Slemish Mountain in County Antrim. The nine Ulster counties are:

Antrim	Donegal	Tyrone
Armagh	Down	
Cavan	Fermanagh	
Derry	Monaghan	

PROMOTING IRISH LANDMARKS

Ireland is one natural island entity in geographical terms, and this is recognised by organisations such as Fáilte Ireland* and Tourism Ireland* that seek to promote the many landmarks that exist across the island.

In political terms, Ireland was partitioned in 1921, following the War of Independence (1919–21) and the passing of the Government of Ireland Act, which became law on 3 May 1921. The six north-eastern counties of Ulster became known as the 'north', or Northern Ireland, which was part of the United Kingdom of Great Britain and Northern Ireland (UK) and the remaining twenty-six counties became the 'south', later Éire and later again the Republic of Ireland.

It was not until 18 April 1949 (Easter Monday) that the 'south' became independent and officially known as the 'Republic of Ireland'. Under the Irish Constitution the country is now known simply as Ireland, or *Éire* in the Irish language, while six of the Ulster counties form Northern Ireland.

The legacy of partition is a complex and often difficult narrative, but this book seeks to portray an array of Irish landmarks, irrespective of what side of the Irish border they are located. In many cases, there are landmarks that straddle both sides, such as the River Erne.

*Fáilte Ireland is the National Tourism Development Authority, whose role is to support the Irish tourism industry and work to sustain Ireland as a high-quality and competitive tourism destination. Fáilte Ireland promotes Ireland as a holiday destination through their domestic marketing campaign (www.discoverireland.ie) and manage a network of nationwide tourist information centres that provide help and advice for visitors to Ireland.

*Tourism Ireland is responsible for marketing the island of Ireland overseas as a holiday and business tourism destination. It was established as one of the 'six areas of co-operation' under the framework of the Good Friday Agreement of 1998. Its remit is to increase tourism to the island of Ireland and to support Northern Ireland to realise its tourism potential.

1

ICONIC COASTAL LANDMARKS, ISLANDS AND LIGHTHOUSES

From Malin Head in the far north to Mizen Head in the far south, the Irish coastline is a treasure trove as far as landmarks are concerned. The Ordnance Survey of Ireland estimates the total length of coastline around the island to be 3,171 kilometres (1,970 miles).

Apart from the many beautiful headlands, peninsulas and beaches located along the coastline such as the Dingle Peninsula in County Kerry and Marble Hill Beach in County Donegal, there are some man-made landmarks that have caught the attention of *munitir na háite* (local people of the area) and visitors alike. These include the marvellous Mussenden Temple in County Antrim, and the iconic Hook Head Lighthouse in County Wexford. Here is a look at these and many other coastal landmarks.

ISLANDS

Ireland itself is an island in the North Atlantic, and it is surrounded by approximately eighty islands of significant size. Only about twenty of these are inhabited, but there are hundreds of other smaller islets dotted around the Irish coast: in the Irish Sea on the eastern coast; and in the Atlantic Ocean to the west and north and the Celtic Sea to the south.

Many of these larger islands are landmarks in their own right. Here is a look at some of those in a clockwise direction starting with Rathlin Island in the north-east of Ireland:

County Antrim
Rathlin Island (*Oileán Reachlainn*)

Located 9.65 kilometres (6 miles) from Ballycastle on the north coast of County Antrim – and only 25.7 kilometres (16 miles) from the Mull of Kintyre in Scotland – Rathlin measures about 14.2 square kilometres (5.5 square miles).

This proximity to Scotland led to disputes over Rathlin's ownership – and was finally settled in 1617 by a unique test: if a snake could survive on the island, it would be taken as being part of Scotland; if it died then Ireland would own it. The snake did not survive!

Rathlin has at times had a difficult history, surviving three massacres and the famine of 1846. Local stories tell of 300 islanders leaving on the same day during that year. Rathlin gave shelter to numerous famous figures, including Robert the Bruce, who hid there after being defeated by the English at Perth in 1306. While hidden in a cave in Rathlin, he drew inspiration from a spider, which tried seven times to bridge the gap between two rocks.

There are many legends associated with the island, including one about an enchanted island that appears from the sea once every seven years. The legend suggests that if you lift a stone from under your feet in Rathlin and throw it onto the island, then it will never disappear again.

County Dublin
Lambay Island

Lambay derives from Old Norse meaning 'lamb island', and lies off the coast of north County Dublin. It is the largest island off the east coast of Ireland (and the most easterly point). In AD 795 the first ever raid by the Vikings on Ireland happened on this island.

Lambay is of note for its diversity of breeding seabirds. The populations of cormorant, herring gull and guillemot are the largest in Ireland and the puffin colony is the only known one on the east coast.

Ireland's Eye (*Inis Mac Neasáin*)

An early Christian monastic site, Ireland's Eye is a small, uninhabited island off the coast of County Dublin, situated directly north of Howth Harbour. Around AD 700 three sons of St Nessan established a monastery here. The church became known as *Cill Mac Nesáin* from which the island got its name in Irish. The 'Garland of Howth' is a fragment of a medieval Irish gospel book, now kept in Trinity College Dublin. It was written at the monastery on Ireland's Eye and is believed to date from the late ninth to early tenth centuries.

Cill Mac Nesáin ceased to function as a church in the thirteenth century, and is now in ruins. In the early nineteenth century a Martello Tower was built on the island to defend against attack from Napoleon's France.

County Wexford
Saltee Islands

The Saltee Islands, the 90-hectare (22-acre) Great Saltee and the 40-hectare (98-acre) Little Saltee lie 4.8 kilometres (3 miles) off Kilmore Quay on the south coast at County Wexford, where an arched deposit of rocks connects the smaller of the two islands to the mainland. The islands were once the haunt of privateers and smugglers, but now they are one of Europe's most important bird sanctuaries. There are also monuments and references to Prince Michael of Saltee on the island. He bought the island in 1943 and crowned himself prince in 1972.

County Cork
Cape Clear Island (*Oileán Cléire*)

Cape Clear is one of only two Gaeltacht (an area where Irish is the predominant language) in County Cork. There is the ruin of a lighthouse on the island, which was the main landfall light for ships arriving from America during most of the nineteenth century.One of Clear Island's historic ruins is *Dún an Óir* (Fort of Gold) established by the O'Driscoll clan.

The Fastnet Rock

Located south of Cape Clear Island, this is the most southerly point of land in Ireland – it was known locally as the 'Teardrop of Ireland', as the lighthouse was often the last bit of Ireland emigrants would see en route to North America.

Dursey Island (*Oileán Baoi*)

Translated from Viking Norse as 'Island of the Bull', Dursey Island, at 6.5 kilometres (4 miles) long and 1.5 kilometres (0.93 miles) wide, lies at the south-western tip of the Beara Peninsula in the west of County Cork. It is one of the few inhabited islands that lie off the south-west coast of Ireland. Dursey Island is notable for the cable car suspended 26 metres (85 feet) above the waves that travels across its narrow sound and connects it to the mainland. It can transport six people, ten sheep or one cow!

County Kerry
Skellig Islands (*Na Scealaga*)
The Skelligs, better known as Sceilig Mhichíl (Great Skellig) and Sceilig Beag (Little Skellig), rise from the Atlantic Ocean 10 kilometres (6 miles) west off the coast of Portmagee.

While there are two islands, it is the larger one that grabs all the headlines. Sceilig Mhichíl was founded in the sixth century and is a site of monastic settlement of the early-Christian period, attracting large numbers of pilgrims and tourists annually. It is the westernmost sacred site along a long line of ancient pilgrimage places running from the west of Ireland through France, Italy and Greece, and then onto Mount Carmel in Palestine.

The first known historical reference to the island comes from the end of the fifth century AD when the King of Munster fled to Sceilig Mhichíl, while the *Annals of Inisfallen* record a Viking attack in AD 823.

Sceilig Mhichíl was uninhabited prior to the foundation of its Christian monastery on the island, estimated to have been between the sixth and eighth centuries. The first recorded reference to monastic activity on the island is a record of the death of 'Suibhini of Skelig' dating from the eighth century. However, St Fionán is claimed to have founded the monastery in the sixth century.

The island was dedicated to St Michael somewhere between 950 and 1050. It was customary to build a new church to celebrate a dedication, and this date fits well with the architectural style of the oldest part of the existing church, known as St Michael's Church. Incidentally, St Michael was the patron saint of high places and the guardian against the powers of darkness.

The monastic site on the island is located on a terraced shelf 183 metres (600 feet) above sea level, and also contains six beehive cells and two oratories, as well as a large number of stone crosses and slabs. The stone dwellings on the island were all made using a technique known as 'corbelling'. The cells and oratories are all of dry-built corbel construction. Over 100 stone crosses of varying sizes have been recorded on the island. The two largest are highly decorated and are located to the north and south of the Large Oratory.

This detailed cluster of huts, oratories and crosses is located following a steep climb of stone steps. Facing southwards and sheltered from the winds, the site was favoured by ascetic monks desiring to live a remote life.

At a rocky crag located further up on the south peak of Sceilig Mhichíl called the Needle's Eye, is another oratory, though inaccessible today, that was favoured as a pilgrimage destination even after the monks departed the island.

The monastery remained continuously occupied until as late as the thirteenth century. During this time, the climate around Sceilig Mhichíl became cooler and more prone to storms. This, along with changes to the structure of the Irish Church, prompted the community to abandon the island and move to the abbey in Ballinskelligs. The island continued to be venerated as a place of pilgrimage in the following centuries.

In 1826, the owner sold the island to the Corporation for Preserving and Improving the Port of Dublin (later to become the Commissioners of Irish Lights), who built two lighthouses on the Atlantic side, and furthermore established the importance of Sceilig Mhichíl in Ireland's maritime history.

As a result of the extreme remoteness of Sceilig Mhichíl, which has until recently discouraged visitors, the site is exceptionally well preserved. In 1996, UNESCO inscribed the island of Sceilig Mhichíl, along with the remains of the monastery, as a World Heritage Site in recognition of its 'outstanding universal value to humanity'. More recently it was featured in two *Star Wars* films, making it an even more popular destination for tourists.

Valentia Island (*Oileán Dairbhre*)
Located off the Iveragh Peninsula on the south-west Kerry coast, Valentia is 26 square kilometres (10 square miles) in area, making it the third largest island off the coast of Ireland. It is linked to the mainland by the Maurice O'Neill Memorial Bridge.

> **Landmark fact:** The island was the site of one end of the first permanent communications link between Europe and Newfoundland in North America. Transatlantic telegraph cables operated from Valentia Island from 27 July 1866, and were replaced regularly until the 1960s.

Blasket Islands (*Na Blascaodaí*)
The Great Blasket Island, the most westerly point in Europe, is the largest of the group of Blasket Islands located 4.8 kilometres (3 miles) off the tip of the Dingle Peninsula. It is 458 hectares (1,132 acres) in area, being 6.5 kilometres (4 miles) long but very narrow, and rising to 292.6 metres (960 feet).

The Blaskets are famous for their beautiful setting – and their writers. Three of them wrote autobiographies that became literary classics: Tomás Ó Crohan, *The Islandman* (1934); Peig Sayers, *An Old Woman's Reflections* (1978); and Maurice O'Sullivan, *Twenty*

Years A'Growing (1933) – a remarkable literary output from one small, remote island.

There was a gradual exodus from the island during the first half of the twentieth century. At one point in the early part of the century, 215 people lived there. However, by 1953–54, the island was finally abandoned by its last remaining twenty inhabitants.

County Galway
The Aran Islands (*Oileáin Árann*)

The three Aran Islands, while set across the mouth of Galway Bay, are actually closer in distance to County Clare. The earliest inhabitants were the *Fír Bolg*, who later lost the islands to the *Eoghanachta* of Munster. They have had numerous owners since then, including the O'Brien family in the eleventh century. A very distinctive feature of the Aran Islands is their stone walls: approximately 1,600 kilometres (995 miles) of hand-built dry stone walls divide the land.

Inis Mór – 'big island'

Inis Mór is the largest of the three Aran Islands at 3,089 hectares (7,635 acres). There is a saying, 'Next Parish Boston', given it is located on the extremity of Ireland and indeed Europe. It includes the following ancient stone forts among its antiquities:

Dún Aengus Fort

Three ancient forts form an intrinsic part of Inis Mór, and perhaps the most spectacular of these sites is the fort of Dún Aengus – a huge semi-circular ringfort of three concentric enclosures lodged on the edge of cliffs that plunge 90 metres (295 feet) into the Atlantic Ocean.

The name Dún Aengus means Fort of Aengus; and it is named after Aengus of the Fír Bolg, the ancient clan who were said to have ruled Ireland for thirty-seven years before being usurped by the Tuatha Dé Danann. Dún Aengus is protected by remarkable 'chevaux de frise' – defensive stone spikes that once had the intention of deterring unwanted visitors.

Excavations carried out in the 1990s indicated that people had been living at the hilltop from around 1500 BC, with the first walls and dwelling houses being erected around 1100 BC. These excavations revealed significant evidence of prehistoric metalworking, as well as several houses and burial places.

Dún Dúcathair

Another fort on the island is Dún Dúcathair (the Black Fort), which has grown in popularity with tourists over the past few years. This is a promontory fort, and what remains is a massive stone wall, straddling an ever-shrinking headland, precariously placed between cliffs. Late Bronze Age objects such as rings, tools, beads and foodstuffs found on site are now on display in the National Museum of Ireland in Dublin.

Hy Brasil

Sometimes visible west of the cliffs of Inis Mór is the outline of what looks like a mountainous island. This is a mirage, a mythical island called Hy Brasil that features in ancient Aran stories as the Island of the Blessed. Until the sixteenth century, Hy Brasil was actually marked on maps. The island is associated with the high king of the Celtic world, Bresal, who established his court on the island.

Inish Maan (Inis Meáin) Middle Island

The second largest of the islands is 911.3 hectares (2,252 acres) in area. Dún Conchúir (Conor's Fort) is an impressive fort based on this island, and it commands great views. Synge's Chair (named in honour of famous Irish playwright J.M. Synge who spent a number of summers on the island) is a semi-circular stone wall that offers a sheltered spot to gaze towards Inis Mór, just as Synge himself might have done.

Inisheer (Inis Oírr) Island of the East

The smallest of the Aran Islands, measures 464.5 hectares (1,148 acres) in area. There are a number of landmarks on Inis Oírr, such as Creggankeel fort and the fourteenth-century O'Brien's Castle – taken from the O'Briens by the O'Flaherty clan of Connemara in 1582, and which occupies the island's highest point.

St MacDara's Island (Oileán Mhic Dara)

This beautiful island is located 7 kilometres (4.3 miles) south of the entrance to Bertraghboy Bay; the twelfth-century church on the eastern shore of this 24.2-hectare (60-acre) island is on the site of a monastery founded by a sixth-century saint named MacDara. The saint's festival is on 16 July, when pilgrims come to the island from the mainland.

County Mayo
Achill Island (*Oileán Acla*)

Connected to the mainland by a bridge at Achill Sound, Achill is 145 square kilometres (56.5 square miles) in area, making it by far the largest island off the coast of Ireland, and more than four times the size of the second largest island, Inis Mór.

Achill has a history of human settlement that is at least 5,000 years old. The remains of megalithic tombs and monuments suggest settlement by Neolithic man in the third or fourth centuries BC.

The L-shaped island is also the most populous Irish island. The first bridge to connect Achill Island to the County Mayo mainland was built in 1887 at Achill Sound, and was named after the founder of the Irish Land League, Michael Davitt.

One of the possible origins of the name Achill is the Gaelic word *acaill*, meaning eagle. Travellers often remarked on the golden eagles and white-tailed sea eagles on Achill, mainly on the peaks of Croaghaun, a mountain that dominates the western end of the island, although the last reported sighting of an eagle on Achill was in 1912.

Inishglora and the Children of Lír

A much smaller Mayo island to the north of Achill is that of Inishglora. The cairns on the island are said to be the resting places of the Children of Lír. The children, Finola and her brothers Aedh, Conn and Fiachra, were changed into swans by a jealous stepmother, Eva, and changed back into humans hundreds of years later by St Kemoc.

County Sligo

Inishmurray (*Inis Muireadheach*)

This island is located about 6 kilometres (3.7 miles) off the coast of Sligo, and contains a monastic settlement ruin, founded by St Molaise in AD 550. The old monastery is in a good state of preservation, and is surrounded by a stone wall up to 4 metres (13 feet) high which has five entrances leading into the central area. It contains a stone-roofed oratory, and two rocks known as 'the cursing stones', among other features.

County Donegal

Many islands, large and small, are located off the coast of County Donegal, and most are uninhabited.

Arranmore (*Árainn Mhór*)

Of those islands that are inhabited, Arranmore is the largest. Thought to have been populated from the early Iron Age, Arranmore or simply 'Aran' has been a centre of Gaelic culture for centuries. It is 5 kilometres (3 miles) long and 4 kilometres (2.5 miles) wide, making it the largest of a group of little islands located off the Rosses district on Donegal's north-west coast.

One of the more accessible of the Gaeltacht islands, this ensures that it remains popular with visitors who enjoy the short boat journey from Burtonport on the mainland. There are great views of the Rosses district from the island, and visitors can enjoy a circular walk.

Tory Island (*Oileán Thoraí*)

It is thought that Tory may have got its name from the Irish for robber (pirate) – Toraí – and this refers to the first inhabitants of Tory, whose king was Balor, also known as Balor of the Evil Eye. Indeed at the east coast of the island lie the ruins known as Balor's Fort.

Described as the Sentinel of the Atlantic by Samuel Bayne when sighting the island when travelling from New York to Derry in 1902, Tory is located about 11 kilometres (7 miles) off Bloody Foreland on the north-west coast of Donegal.

It is just 4 kilometres (2.5 miles) long and 1.2 kilometres (0.75 miles) wide, but over the years Tory has been recognised as being the most remote and windswept of any of the Irish islands. Links with the past are in evidence on Tory Island, from the Iron Age fort to the impressive remains of the early Celtic Church of St Colmcille.

The island has been inhabited for centuries. In pre-Christian times it was occupied by the Nemedians, said to have come from Ireland from Scythia. Later came the Fomorians who initiated the concept of the 'King of Tory', which exists in present times. It is said that Colmcille brought Christianity to the island and banished the pagans forever, building the church and seven small chapels.

There has been tragedy: popular tradition tells of at least three galleons of the Spanish Armada falling foul of Tory's dangerous rocks and tides in 1588. The earliest identified wreck was the *Jamaica Merchant* in 1744. Ships would continue to collide for the next 300 years, and Tory's most famous shipwreck is that of HMS *Wasp* in 1884, when the ship struck in daylight just near the lighthouse.

The King of Tory Island

Patsy Dan Rodgers' contributions to his island's culture and wellbeing have been recognised by his fellow islanders who bestowed on him the title of King of Tory. He follows in a distinguished line, from the inaugural King Conán the Fomorian.

THE WILD ATLANTIC WAY

The 1,235 kilometres (767 miles) of coastline with its sheltered bays and Blue Flag beaches called the Wild Atlantic Way runs along Ireland's beautiful west coast. Indeed this coastline has some of the most impressive scenery of any part of Ireland. Described by a number of travel writers as 'the longest defined coastal touring route in the world', the Wild Atlantic Way on the west coast of Ireland was officially inaugurated by Fáilte Ireland in 2014.

County Donegal is the designated northern starting point and this road trip traces the coastline from Malin Head on the Inishowen Peninsula – Ireland's most northerly point – to the seaside town of Kinsale in County Cork in the south.

The Wild Atlantic Way has over 160 official discovery points, of which fifteen have been designated as signature discovery points, and these include Dursey Island in County Cork and Skelligs View in County Kerry. Some other landmarks that are popular along the Wild Atlantic Way include:

Cliffs of Moher, County Clare

The Cliffs of Moher are located at the south-western edge of the Burren region. The cliffs take their name from a fort dating back to the first century BC called *Mothar* (meaning 'ruined fort'), which once stood on Hag's Head, the southernmost point of the cliffs.

Stretching for 8 kilometres (5 miles) along the Atlantic coastline of County Clare, the cliffs reach 214 metres (700 feet) at their highest point at Knockardakin. Midway along the cliffs is an impressive visitor centre set into the hillside and opened in 2007.

Close to this is O'Brien's Tower, built in 1835 by the local landowner, Cornelius O'Brien (and a Member of Parliament for County Clare). He built the tower observation point for the hundreds of tourists who even then, visited the cliffs. From the cliffs, visitors can see the Aran Islands in Galway Bay, and it is the marvellous views and sheer beauty of the area that ensures the Cliffs of Moher are among the most visited tourist sites in Ireland. The visitor centre estimated that the area received over 1.25 million visitors in 2015.

> **Landmark fact:** As the dramatic backdrop for many movies, TV series, music videos and adverts, the Cliffs of Moher have become a recognisable landmark on the big screen. Some of the bigger and more recent movies filmed at the Cliffs of Moher include *Harry Potter and the Half- Blood Prince*.

Slieve League Cliffs, County Donegal

Situated on the south-west coast of Donegal, these are among the highest sea cliffs in Europe, and are almost three times the height of the Cliffs of Moher. At 609 metres (1,998 feet) high, views from here include Donegal Bay and surrounding Counties Leitrim, Sligo and Mayo.

To the west is the Atlantic Ocean, and north-west is Rathlin O'Beirne Island and Glencolmcille. On the high slopes of Slieve League there are remains of an early-Christian monastic site, with chapel and beehive huts. There are also ancient stone remains that suggest that the mountain was a site of pilgrimage before the arrival of Christianity.

Landmark fact: During the Second World War, the word *Éire* was placed in large stones on headlands around Donegal, to act as a navigational aid for the Allied planes to fly along what was called the Donegal Corridor. One such sign remains at Slieve League, beside the viewing point car park.

PENINSULAS AND HEADLANDS

Inishowen, County Donegal

The Inishowen Peninsula in County Donegal proudly holds the title of having the northernmost point on the island of Ireland: and that accolade goes to Malin Head. Often referred to as 'a miniature Ireland', Inishowen comprises a marvellous landscape, with beaches (especially Kinnego Bay, Culdaff, Tullagh and Pollan) and the central mountain range, with towering Slieve Snaght at the middle.

The 'Inishowen 100' Scenic Route

Voted one of the top scenic routes in Ireland by the *Irish Independent*, the 'Inishowen 100' is a 100-mile driving route that follows Inishowen's coastline, taking in stunning panoramic views of Lough Swilly, the Atlantic Ocean and Lough Foyle.

Malin Head, County Donegal

The most northerly point of the Wild Atlantic Way – and Ireland – is Malin Head. It's a breathtaking headland, with many attractions along the cliff edge, including a natural arch called the Devil's Bridge.

On a clear day, visitors can see as far as the Scottish coastline, while Tory and Inishtrahull Islands are also visible.

Banba's Crown

The landmark of Ireland's most northerly point is the signal tower on Banba's Crown at Malin Head. Banba was one of the mythical queens of Ireland. This tower was constructed in 1805, during the Napoleonic Wars. Its original purpose was to act as a coastguard, reporting on ships passing along this busy transatlantic route. Banba's Crown was the spot where loved ones waved goodbye to their families and friends as they set out across the sea on the long voyage to a new life in America.

The Old Head of Kinsale, County Cork

The Old Head of Kinsale is a headland near the town of Kinsale in County Cork. An early lighthouse was established in the seventeenth century by Robert Reading, who built several other lighthouses in Ireland. One of Ireland's most spectacular coastal areas, this large promontory juts out into the Atlantic Ocean, rising hundreds of feet above the water with towering sea cliffs.

The Old Head of Kinsale Loop is a gentle 6-kilometre walk that leads to the mysterious ruins of a fort, which is said to have been built by the Celts around 100 BC. Further on, the black and white striped Old Head Lighthouse stands looking out to sea. It was just off the coast here that a German torpedo sank the *Lusitania* – the wreck of which still lies there beneath the waves.

Howth Head, County Dublin

Originally an island, Howth Head is connected to the mainland via a narrow strip of land. A prominent landmark of Dublin Bay, Howth Head is a favourite destination for hikes and walks on the famous Howth Head cliff path.

The peninsula is a bird sanctuary, and boasts numerous attractions, including Ireland's Eye, Howth Castle and a Martello Tower. For fans of James Joyce's celebrated novel *Ulysses*, Howth Head is where Leopold Bloom proposed to Molly.

Iveragh Peninsula, County Kerry

The Iveragh Peninsula is the largest peninsula in south-western Ireland, and is flanked by both Dingle Bay and Kenmare Bay. A mountain range, the Macgillycuddy's Reeks (see Chapter 2), lies in the centre of the peninsula. Some places of note in the Iveragh Peninsula include Killarney National Park, Ross Castle and Muckross House.

The Ring of Kerry

The Ring of Kerry is a predominantly coastal 180-kilometre (122-mile) driving route on the Iveragh Peninsula that begins and ends in Killarney. Towns located along the Ring of Kerry include Cahirciveen and Killorglin.

Mizen Head, County Cork

Mizen Head is located at the extremity of the Kilmore Peninsula in the district of Carbery in County Cork. It is the most south-westerly point in Ireland. 'Malin to Mizen' most commonly refers to a journey from Malin Head (Ireland's most northerly point to Mizen Head (commonly thought to be Ireland's most southerly point).

This journey is most often attempted by cyclists and walkers as a challenge route, with the goal of raising money for charities; the shortest road distance from Malin to Mizen is approximately 611 kilometres (380 miles).

LIGHTHOUSES

Lighthouses have played a crucial role in the safety of ships over the centuries. Ireland's oldest operational lighthouse was built at Hook Head, County Wexford, in the twelfth century. This was apparently on the site where St Dubhan tended a fire beacon on a primitive tower in the fifth century.

County Donegal has a number of well-known lighthouses, including Ireland's most northerly lighthouse, Inishtrahull, off the coast of Malin Head:

Inishtrahull, County Donegal
The first lighthouse was built on the east end of the island around 1812. Its light was visible up to a distance of 30 kilometres (19 miles). The present tower was built in 1958 at the west end of the island, and is Ireland's most northerly lighthouse.

Fanad Head, County Donegal
Established on St Patrick's Day 1817 (designed by one of the foremost civil engineers of the time, George Halpin), Fanad Head Lighthouse was established after the frigate HMS *Saldanha* was wrecked there several years previously. It is now a helicopter base for Tory Island and Inishtrahull. Standing between idyllic Lough Swilly and sandy Mulroy Bay, its location within the Donegal Gaeltacht on the eastern shore of the Fanad Peninsula is a highlight of the Wild Atlantic Way.

Rathlin, County Antrim
Known as Ireland's only 'upside-down' lighthouse; the lighthouse was built into the cliff face between 1912 and 1917. A special pier and an inclined railway from the pier to the clifftop had to be built to facilitate the lighthouse's construction.

Lightkeepers lived in the lighthouse until it was automated in 1983. It is one of seventy lighthouses operated by the Commissioners of Irish Lights around the coast of Ireland and continues to play a vital role in maritime safety today.

Blackhead Lighthouse, County Antrim

Blackhead Lighthouse surveys the sea from the edge of a majestic cliff on Belfast Lough. This lighthouse was built and its light first exhibited in 1902. Its light would have guided many famous vessels during Belfast's golden age of shipping, including the ill-fated *Titanic*.

St John's Point, County Down

Its strikingly tall tower is marked with vibrant bands of yellow and black (the colours that distinguish it from other lighthouses are known as its 'daymark'). St John's Point Lighthouse was designed by George Halpin Senior, one of the most famous civil engineers of the time. The light was first exhibited in 1844.

Landmark fact: St John's Point has a curious connection to the Irish playwright Brendan Behan. Behan's father was contracted to paint a number of lighthouses across Ireland and enlisted Brendan to paint St John's Point in 1950.

Wicklow Head, County Wicklow

Wicklow Head Lighthouse has overlooked the scenic coastline since 1781; it was one of two lighthouses built on the headland that year. The original light source was twenty tallow candles set against a large mirror reflector.

On 10 October 1836 lightning struck the historic tower, and the interior was destroyed. The 95ft-high stone tower once supported an eight-sided lantern and has been renovated by the Irish Landmark Trust as a unique place to stay for visitors.

Hook Lighthouse, County Wexford

Hook Lighthouse is truly unique. Located at the tip of Hook Head a few kilometres from the village of Slade, it was built some time between 1210 and 1230. The lighthouse continues to serve its original function and is now one of the oldest operational lighthouses in the world – a beacon having been here since the fifth century.

William Marshal built the lighthouse tower to protect ships entering Waterford Harbour. Marshal also founded the town of New Ross at the confluence of the Rivers Barrow and Nore.

The monks of St Saviour's of Rinndeaun, a monastery founded by a Welsh monk called St Dubhán in the fifth century, looked after the lighthouse tower for almost 400 years. Remarkably lightkeepers and their families lived at the lighthouse until 1977.

Loop Head, County Clare

Loop Head Lighthouse is perched at the end of Loop Head Peninsula in west County Clare. There has been a lighthouse at Loop Head since 1670. Originally it was a coal-burning brazier on a platform on the roof of the cottage lighthouse where the lightkeeper lived. The first tower lighthouse was built in 1802 and was replaced by a new tower in 1854. The lighthouse converted to electric operation in 1971 and was automated in 1991.

AND FINALLY...

Two very famous coastal landmarks located on the north-east coast of Ireland, not far from each other:

Giant's Causeway, County Antrim

The Giant's Causeway is steeped in myth and legend. Some say it was carved from the coast by the mighty giant, Fionn Mac Cumhaill, so as to avoid getting his feet wet while walking between Ireland and the coast of Scotland en route to fight his Scottish counterpart

Benandonner. Apparent clues of his existence – including the Giant's Boot and Wishing Chair – are considered intrinsic parts of the Causeway.

Sixty million years ago, this area was subject to intense volcanic activity, when highly fluid molten rock was forced up through fissures in the chalk bed to form an extensive lava plateau. The dramatic cliff-like edge of the plateau forms the Causeway coastline. The larger fissures, through which the lava flowed, can be clearly seen as bands of dark rock, which cut down the cliff faces and jut out to sea. There were three periods of volcanic activity which resulted in the flows, known as the Lower, Middle and Upper Basalts.

It is the Middle Basalts rock which forms the columns of the Giants Causeway. The rapidly cooling lava contracted and variations in the cooling rate resulted in the world famous columnar structure. Indeed, the formation consists of about 40,000 interlocking basalt columns, most of which are hexagonal. The columns form huge stepping-stones, some as high as 12 metres (39 feet), which slope down to the sea.

These giant basalt columns have been attracting numerous visitors since they were first discovered by the Victorians. The novelist Walter Scott selected four of them to take home with him but was convinced to change his mind! In terms of international recognition, the Giant's Causeway was granted the status of a World Heritage Site in 1986 by the United Nations Educational, Scientific and Cultural Organisation (UNESCO).

The Causeway area is owned and managed for the National Trust. The Causeway Coast area has been designated as an Area of Outstanding Natural Beauty (AONB); this 30-kilometre (17-mile) route extends from Ramore Head at Portrush, eastwards along the north Antrim coast to near Ballycastle. There are many other notable landmarks in this area, such as Dunluce Castle (see Chapter 5).

Landmark fact: The causeway was home to Europe's first ever hydro-electric tram which was open for sixty-five years from 1883. Part of the route was reopened in the spring of 2002.

Mussenden Temple, County Derry

Another famous coastal landmark is located less than 32 kilometres (20 miles) from the Giant's Causeway. Built in 1785, Mussenden Temple is located in the beautiful surroundings of Downhill Demesne, near Castlerock in County Derry, and is protected by the National

Trust. It perches dramatically on a 36-metre (120-foot) cliff top, high above the Atlantic Ocean, offering spectacular views westwards over Downhill Strand towards Magilligan Point.

The eighteenth-century Earl of Bristol (and Church of Ireland Bishop of Derry), Frederick Augustus Hervey, created an estate at Downhill. Hervey spent a considerable sum on the house and gardens, erecting a series of neoclassical buildings in the grounds, including the Mussenden Temple.

Its classic domed rotunda was apparently modelled on the Temple of Vesta at Tivoli near Rome and originally designed as a summer library, built for Hervey's niece – Frideswide Mussenden Bruce. The temple, which was to have been her refuge, became her memorial when she died in 1785. The inscription on the temple translates as: 'It is agreeable to watch, from land, someone else involved in a great struggle while winds whip up the waves out at sea.'

Over the years this temple was in danger of being lost to the sea, due to the erosion of the cliff which brought Mussenden Temple ever closer to the edge. In 1997, the National Trust carried out cliff stabilisation work to prevent the loss of this famous coastal landmark.

2

HILLS AND MOUNTAINS

HILLS

Due to Ireland's 'saucer-like' topography, the majority of its higher upland areas are to be found in the coastal counties. There are some very famous hills – landmarks in their own right – that have associations with important events in Irish history. Here is a selection of them:

Hill of Tara, County Meath
The iconic Hill of Tara is known in Irish as *Teamhair na Ríogh*, High Place of the Kings, although another interpretation of the name Tara says that it means 'a place of great prospect'. Although a little over 91 metres (300 feet) in height and spanning around 40.5 hectares (100 acres), Tara still commands the surrounding countryside, and indeed on a clear day it is claimed that half the counties of Ireland can be seen from Tara.

It is one of the most famous sacred landmarks in the country – in terms of ancient Irish religion and mythology. Tara was revered as a dwelling of the gods and an entrance place to the other world of eternal joy, where it was believed that no mortal ever grew old.

There are several monuments famous in mythology, dating from the Stone Age and later. Most of the sites at Tara were given names by nineteenth-century antiquarians. The *Ráth na Seanad* (Fort of the Kings) consists of a set of concentric banks surrounding a flat-topped mound covering burial sites. Two gold torcs were found nearby in the early eighteenth century.

Duma na nGiall ('Mound of the Hostages') is a passage grave that sits within the fort. This is the oldest monument on the site, being built around 3000 BC. Named after Niall of the Nine Hostages, this was excavated during the 1950s and has been dated back to 3500 BC. It is aligned with sunrise on the festivals of Samhain (beginning of winter) and Imbolc (beginning of spring).

Another mound, named the *Forradh*, is topped with the *Lia Fáil* (the 'Stone of Destiny') which legend said would cry out when the rightful King of Ireland placed his foot upon it. There are 142 kings believed to have ruled there from prehistory up to Brian Boru, who died in AD 1014. The *Lia Fáil* coronation stone was brought by the Tuatha Dé Danann and has rested here down the ages. Cormac Mac Airt was one of the most famous High Kings of Tara and is said to have ruled for forty years.

The present church building and churchyard at Tara date from 1822. There were two previous churches on the hill. The first one was built in the thirteenth century and a much larger church succeeded it. The churchyard has a number of historic features, including two standing stones, known in legend as Bloc and Bligne, which are said to have played a part in the royal inauguration ceremonies.

> **Landmark fact:** Tara has been involved in some of the most crucial episodes in Irish history. The site was prominent during the 1798 Rising, when the Battle of Tara took place between the United Irishmen and British forces on 26 May. Daniel O'Connell held a 'Monster Meeting' at Tara which is estimated to have attracted half a million people!

Cavehill, County Antrim

Cave Hill is a basaltic hill that stands 368 metres (1,207 feet) above sea level to the north of Belfast, overlooking Belfast Lough. It is known in Irish as *Beann Mhadagáin*, meaning 'Madagán's Peak' – named after a King of Ulster who died in AD 856, but gets its English name from five caves that are located on the side of the main Belfast cliffs.

It is distinguished by its famous 'Napoleon's Nose', a feature that resembles the profile of the famous French Emperor Napoleon. Nearby attractions such as Cave Hill Country Park, Belfast Zoo and Belfast Castle are popular with locals and tourists alike who marvel at the beauty of Cave Hill looming in the background.

The Cave Hill summit offers stunning views over Belfast towards other landmarks such as the Mourne Mountains, and Scrabo Tower in County Down can be seen on a clear day. Culturally, Cave Hill has long been a landmark of great significance and is thought to be the inspiration for Jonathan Swift's *Gulliver's Travels*. Swift thought that the hill resembled the shape of a sleeping giant safeguarding the city.

Hill of Allen, County Kildare

The Hill of Allen, or *Cnoc Alúine*, is a volcanic hill situated in the west of County Kildare, near the village of Allen. According to Irish mythology it is associated with legendary warrior Fionn Mac Cumhaill and the Fianna. The hill is situated at the easternmost point of the Bog of Allen and it is from this hill that the bog gets its name. The Hill of Allen commands an extensive view of the Wicklow and Slieve Bloom mountains, as well as the Curragh plains.

According to legend, Fionn Mac Cumhaill had a fortress on the hill and used the surrounding flatlands as training grounds for his warriors, while in AD 722 the Battle of Allen was fought in close proximity to the hill between the King of Leinster and the forces of the High King of Ireland.

A small mound called *Suidh Fionn*, Finn's Chair, occupies the highest point, and in its centre stands the tower of Allen (completed in 1863), and this is known locally as Aylmer's Folly, as it was the idea of Sir Gerald George Aylmer of Donadea Castle. When digging the foundations the workmen discovered a cave, 2.7 metres (9 feet) deep, filled with soft clay, at the bottom of which they came upon a remarkably large human skeleton, which they believed was that of the giant Fionn Mac Cumhaill.

Hill of Uisneach, County Westmeath

The Hill of Uisneach was one of the great ceremonial sites of late prehistoric Ireland. In mythology, Uisneach is the meeting place of the five ancient provinces of Ireland – Connacht, Leinster, Munster, Ulster and *Mide*. The Irish word *Mide* means 'neck' and this fifth province may be regarded as the means of joining head to body, and body to soul.

This landmark, located on the road to Ballymore, about 14.5 kilometres (9 miles) west of Mullingar, is traditionally identified as the 'middle of Ireland' (although the actual geographical centre of Ireland is near the western shore of Lough Ree, further to the west) and consists of the remains of over two dozen archaeological monuments, including a megalithic tomb, burial mounds, standing stones, enclosures and ringforts.

Uisneach is often associated with the beginning of the fire festival of Bealtaine (1 May) as it was the home of the Fire Druids and hosted a major celebration of Bealtaine in times past. Uisneach is the sacred site of the ancient goddess, *Ériu*, from which Ireland gets her name.

In ancient times the land was seen as the embodiment of the goddess – the rocks were her bones, the earth her flesh and the rivers her veins. An annual festival was held in her honour at Bealtaine, and according to tradition all the fires in Ireland were extinguished on that evening and two great bonfires were lit on top of the sacred hill as a beacon, a symbol of *Ériu*'s eyes looking out over the horizons.

A famous feature of Uisneach is the Cat Stone, often called the *Aill na Míreann* (the Stone of the Divisions), as it is said to have been where the borders of the provinces met. This fissured and fragmenting limestone boulder stands on the south-west slopes of the Hill of Uisneach, and has five faces, each looking towards one of the ancient provinces.

Although the Hill of Uisneach stands just 181 metres (596 feet) above sea level, its summit commands extensive panoramic views over the central plain, with no less than twenty counties visible on the horizon. It was on the summit that the palace of King Tuathal Techtmar stood in the second century AD, and it is believed that the high kings of Ireland ruled for two centuries until the seat moved back to Tara.

Mount Pelier Hill and the Hell Fire Club, County Dublin

This 383-metre (1,257-foot) high hill is a member of the 'Dublin Group' of mountains and is commonly referred to as the Hell Fire Club, the popular name given to the ruined building at the summit. This building was a hunting lodge constructed by the Speaker of the Irish House of Commons William Conolly (see Castletown, Chapter 4) around 1725, and was originally named Mount Pelier – and since its construction the hill has also gone by the same name.

The surrounding landscape has prehistoric remains, including a cairn from which stones were removed to help build Mount Pelier Lodge. Soon after the building was completed, a massive storm blew the roof off. Immediately, rumours circulated that this had been the work of the Devil – the payback for stealing the stones.

The hill has become associated with various paranormal events, and this has been linked to the Hell Fire Club that was founded around 1737 by Richard Parsons and James Worsdale. The club rented the lodge and engaged in the occult. The ruins of the hunting lodge is haunted by a huge black cat – the symbol of the Hellfire Club.

MOUNTAINS

Some mountains in Ireland extend across a number of counties, such as the Sperrin Mountains (Derry and Tyrone); and some to the sea, such as the Mourne Mountains. One of the most famous mountains in Ireland is Slemish Mountain as it has been closely linked to St Patrick, the patron saint of Ireland. Here is a look at some of the landmark mountains in Ireland listed according to each province, along with a little background on each:

Ulster
Sperrin Mountains, Counties Derry and Tyrone
Na Speirín means 'pointed hills' and, spanning 64 kilometres (40 miles), the Sperrins mountain range is the largest in Ireland. The Sperrins region is a designated Area of Outstanding Natural Beauty (AONB) by the Department of Agriculture, Environment and Rural Affairs in Northern Ireland. The wider Sperrins area stretches across North Tyrone from the border with Derry to Lough Neagh in the east, taking in a large part of east Tyrone.

Sawel Mountain is the highest peak in the Sperrins, with a summit rising to 678 metres (2,175 feet). It has the honour of being the County Top for both Derry and Tyrone as it straddles and marks the Tyrone–Derry boundary. Another of the Sperrins, Carntogher at 464 metres (1,522 feet), towers over the Glenshane Pass in County Derry.

Motorists can experience one of the Sperrins' four scenic driving routes – covering the Central, South, East and North Sperrins scenic routes. These were included in *National Geographic*'s list of the top scenic drives for 2012.

Among the Sperrins' best-known landmarks is the Beaghmore Stone Circle in County Tyrone (see Chapter 6).

Mount Errigal and the 'Poisoned Glen', County Donegal
The mountains of County Donegal consist of two main ranges – the Derryveagh Mountains in the north and the Bluestack Mountains in the south. The western part of the Derryveagh range contains Mount Errigal. The name derives from the Irish *Aireagál*, meaning 'oratory'.

At 751 metres (2,464 feet) it is the highest in Donegal and the second highest in the province of Ulster. Mount Errigal is certainly among the most climbed mountains, despite its remote location. Errigal has the magical quality of appearing to change shape, depending on what direction you view it from.

'One Man's Pass' is located at the summit of Mount Errigal, joining the twin summits approximately 30 to 40 metres (98 to 131 feet) apart, and from this height the visitor will see the 'Poisoned Glen' in all its glory.

Lost in translation?
The 'Poisoned Glen' is renowned for its sweeping valleys, imposing mountains and lakes, and was originally known by the local people as the 'heavenly glen'. Unfortunately, an error was made by an English

cartographer during translation when he confused the Irish word for heaven (*neamh*) with the word for poison (*neimhe*).

Slemish Mountain, County Antrim

Slemish Mountain, the legendary first known Irish home of St Patrick, is located in County Antrim. The mountain rises about 437 metres (1,433 feet) above the surrounding plain, and it is actually the central core of an extinct volcano.

For miles around Ballymena, the landscape is dominated by this superb natural landmark. Excellent views can be enjoyed of the Antrim and Scottish coasts to the east. Ballymena town, Lough Neagh and the Sperrin Mountains are all normally visible to the west, while the Bann Valley and the higher summits of the Antrim Hills can be seen to the north. Indeed, Slemish itself can clearly be seen from the summit of Tulach Óg Fort in east Tyrone (Chapter 6) almost 48 kilometres (30 miles) away.

St Patrick and Slemish

According to legend, following his capture and being brought as a slave to Ireland, Patrick herded sheep and pigs at Slemish Mountain for about six years, from the age of 16, for a man named Milchu.

It was during this time that Patrick turned to frequent prayer as his only consolation in his loneliness. In a vision he was encouraged to escape and return home. He did, and after years of religious study to become a priest and missionary, Patrick dreamed of returning to Ireland.

Pope Celestine fulfilled his wish and commissioned him as bishop to preach the gospel to the Celtic people. He led a religious mission across Ireland, preaching and baptising, ordaining priests and bishops, erecting churches and establishing places of learning and worship.

Slemish Mountain is open year-round, and on St Patrick's Day (17 March) large crowds hike to the top of the mountain as a pilgrimage.

Mourne Mountains, County Down

The Mourne Mountains are a granite mountain range in County Down, and includes the highest mountains in the province of Ulster. The highest of these is Slieve Donard at 850 metres (2,788 feet). The Mournes have also been designated as an Area of Outstanding Natural Beauty (AONB). The name Mourne is derived from the name of a Gaelic clann or sept called the *Múghdhorna*.

Mourne Landmarks

The Mourne Wall is among the more famous features in the Mournes. It is a 35-kilometre (21-mile) drystone wall that crosses fifteen summits and was constructed to define the boundaries of the area of land purchased by the Belfast Water Commissioners in the late nineteenth century. Construction of the Mourne Wall was started in 1904 and was completed in 1922.

Some of the Mourne Mountains have names beginning with 'Slieve', from the Irish word *sliabh*, meaning 'mountain'. One example is Slieve Donard:

Slieve Donard

Ulster's highest peak, Slieve Donard is the tallest of the Mourne Mountains. Located just south of Newcastle, County Down, it is estimated to be 852 metres (2,796 feet) tall.

The Mourne Wall passes over fifteen mountains, including Slieve Donard. It runs up the western and southern slopes of the mountain, joining a small stone tower at the summit. Also on the summit are the remains of two prehistoric burial cairns, one of which is the remains of the highest known passage tomb in Ireland. In Irish mythology the mountain was associated with, and named after, the mythical figures Boirche and Slángha.

It was later associated with, and named after, St Donard, who was said to have made the summit his hermitage. Up until the 1830s, people made a pilgrimage to the mountaintop in late July each year.

In 1826, the Royal Engineers used Slieve Donard as a base to map Ireland. They camped on the mountaintop from late July until late

November that year and used the two cairns to make triangulation points. During the survey two men died in a snowstorm on their way down the mountain and others were injured during storms on the summit.

> **Landmark fact:** In 1896, the Irish musician and artist Percy French wrote a song entitled *The Mountains of Mourne* that offers an account of the landmark from the nostalgic viewpoint of an Irish labourer from a village near the mountains.

Slieve Gullion, County Armagh

Derived from the Irish *Sliabh gCuillinn* which means 'mountain of the steep slope', it is located in the south of County Armagh. It is the highest point in the county, with an elevation of 577 metres (1,894 feet). Slieve Gullion is a steep volcanic mass surrounded by a rocky ridge about 13 kilometres (8 miles) across, known as the Ring of Gullion, another designated Area of Outstanding Natural Beauty (AONB).

This ring marks the edge of a massive explosion some 60 million years ago. From the top of Slieve Gullion this 'ring' can be seen as a circle of twelve small granite hills. At the summit is a small lake, known as the Lake of Sorrow, or the *Calliag Bheara's* lake. The *Calliag* was a witch, and she has associations with other peaks, such as the hills of Loughcrew in County Meath. There are also two ancient burial cairns on top of the mountain. The southern cairn is a large passage grave – the highest surviving passage grave in Ireland.

The mountain of Slieve Gullion plays a prominent role in the mythology and history of the area. It is mentioned many times in the ancient Irish battle epic, the *Tain Bó Cuailnge*, as *Sliabh gCuillinn*, and according to mythology, the mountain is named after Culann the metalsmith.

Connacht
Benbulben, County Sligo

The flat–topped profile of Benbulben (translated as Jaw's Peak) rises spectacularly from Sligo's coastal plains to its 526-metre (1,726-foot) summit overlooking Donegal Bay. Its profile changes constantly as you travel round it, and it is noted in Irish mythology for being the location where Fionn Mac Cumhaill found his son Óisín on the mountainside, having searched for him for seven years.

Another legend surrounding Benbulben is that this is the only place in Ireland where fairies are also visible to mortals. Benbulben is believed to have a 'fairy door' on the east side of its north face – so whenever the door opens, the weather in the area is good for the next few days.

Croagh Patrick, County Mayo

Croagh Patrick, which overlooks Clew Bay and is located near the town of Westport in County Mayo, is considered the holiest mountain in Ireland. Croagh Patrick comes from the Irish *Cruach Phádraig* meaning St Patrick's Stack.

Long before St Patrick's arrival, the mountain was known by its ancient name of *Cruchán Aigli*. Nowadays it is known locally as the Reek, a reference to its distinctive conical shape. It is the third highest peak in Mayo, after Mweelrea and Nephin and rises to a summit of 750 metres (2,460 feet).

The tradition of pilgrimage to this holy mountain stretches back over 5,000 years from the Stone Age to the present day, without interruption. Its religious significance dates back to pagan times, when people are thought to have gathered here to celebrate the beginning of the harvest season.

Croagh Patrick is renowned for its Patrician Pilgrimage in honour of St Patrick. It was on the summit of the mountain that St Patrick fasted for forty days in AD 44 and the custom has been faithfully handed down from generation to generation. Each year, the Reek attracts about 1 million pilgrims. On 'Reek Sunday', the last Sunday in July, over 25,000 pilgrims visit the mountain. Traditionally, people from Westport make the pilgrimage two days before, on Garland Friday.

> **Landmark fact:** At the top of Croagh Patrick, there is a chapel that was built in 1905 by local men who brought all the materials up the side of the mountain transported by donkeys.

Twelve Bens, County Galway

The Twelve Bens (also known as 'The Twelve Pins') is a range of sharp-peaked mountains located north-east of Roundstone in Connemara, County Galway. They take in many of the highest mountains in the west of Ireland, and the highest point in the Twelve Bens is Benbaun at 729 metres (2,392 feet). Topographically, this range is partnered with the Maumturks range on the other side of the lonely Glen Inagh.

Leinster
Cooley Mountains, County Louth
The mountains that occupy the Carlingford or Cooley Peninsula in north County Louth are known as the Cooley Mountains. Slieve Foye at 588 metres (1,930 feet) is the highest peak on the eastern ridge and the highest peak in County Louth.

The ridge rises at the Foxes Rock 404 metres (1,325 feet), and runs for roughly 6 kilometres (3.5 miles) in a south-easterly direction to the town of Carlingford. The entire ridge is known as Carlingford Mountain.

The Cooley Mountains are a very popular destination for hill walkers. The famous Táin Way, which is a national walking route, covers 40 kilometres (25 miles) of the Cooley Mountains.

Poc Fada
For more than half a century, the All-Ireland *Poc Fada* competition has taken place over the Cooley Mountains. The *Poc Fada* (meaning 'long puck') is a hurling competition where contestants have to hit the *sliotar* (ball) as far as they possibly can over a particular course.

The concept of the competition originates in the Irish legend of Táin Bó Cuailgne, when Cúchulainn, who as the boy Setanta set out from his home to the king's court at Emain Macha (see Chapter 6) hitting his *sliotar* before him and running ahead to catch it.

The tournament was founded in 1960 by Fr Pól Mac Sheáin and the Naomh Moninne Club based in Dundalk, County Louth. The course is 5 kilometres (3 miles) in length and the winner is the person to cover the course in the least number of pucks. All-Ireland gold, silver and bronze medals are presented to the winners.

Slieve Bloom Mountains, Counties Laois and Offaly
The Slieve Bloom Mountains rise from the central plains of Ireland to a height of 527 metres (1,730 feet). The highest points are Arderin 527 metres (1,730 feet) at the south-western end of the range and Baunreaghcong 511 metres (1,676 feet) at the end of the Ridge of Capard.

The Slieve Bloom Mountains form a natural link between County Laois and County Offaly. Along with the Massif Central in France, the Slieve Bloom Mountains are the oldest mountains in Europe; they were once also the highest at 3,700 metres (12,138 feet), but weathering has reduced them to 527 metres (1,730 feet).

Munster
MacGillycuddy's Reeks, County Kerry
The MacGillycuddy's Reeks is a mountain range that stretches out along the Iveragh Peninsula that contains Carrauntoohil *Corrán Tuathail* – the tallest mountain in Ireland at 1,040 metres (3,414 feet). Occupying about 100 square kilometres (38.6 square miles), the range stretches from the picturesque Gap of Dunloe in the east to Glencar in the west.

MacGillycuddy's Reeks (Irish *Na Cruacha Dubha* meaning 'the black stacks') is a mountain range that includes nine of Ireland's twelve summits that exceed 900 metres (2,952 feet) in altitude. The ridge northwards leads to Ireland's second highest peak, Beenkeragh, 1,038 metres (3,405 feet), while the ridge westward leads to the third highest peak, Caher, 1,001 metres (3,284 feet).

The name of the range dates to the eighteenth century, when the *Mac Giolla Mochuda* (anglicised MacGillycuddy) clan were local landowners. The clan chief, MacGillycuddy of the Reeks, owned land in this part of Munster for a long time prior, and continued to do so until the end of the twentieth century. The MacGillycuddys were a cadet branch of the O'Sullivans, once one of the most powerful families in Munster.

A wooden cross was erected on the summit in the 1950s by the local community, and was replaced by a 5-metre (16-foot) tall steel cross in 1976. Carrauntoohil attracts thousands of enthusiastic walkers each year. They are said to have reached Heaven's Gateway at the pinnacle of the mountain.

Galtee Mountains, Counties Cork, Limerick and Tipperary
The Galtee Mountains are Ireland's highest inland mountain range and are spread across the borders of three counties in Munster – Limerick, Tipperary and Cork.

The name for this range of mountains was derived from the Irish *Sléibhte na gCoillte*, or 'Mountains of the Forests'. Galtymore is the highest peak in the range, reaching 917 metres (3,009 feet). Outside of County Kerry, Galtymore is the highest peak in the province of Munster. It is situated about halfway between Mitchelstown and Tipperary Town on the Tipperary–Limerick border.

The Glen of Aherlow is a lush valley where the River Aherlow runs between the Galtee Mountains and the wooded ridge of Slievenamuck. Bounded by the rural villages of Bansha and Galbally, this glen was historically an important pass between Counties Limerick and Tipperary.

Within the glen the focal point is the statue of Christ the King. Erected in 1950, Christ the King overlooks the valley at its most scenic viewpoint, has his hand raised, 'blessing the Glen and all who pass by', and attracts thousands of visitors every year. The entrance to the Glen of Aherlow Nature Park is adjacent to Christ the King.

Knockmealdown Mountains, Counties Tipperary and Waterford

The Knockmealdown Mountains, *Sléibhte Chnoc Mhaoldomhnaigh* is a mountain range located on the border of Counties Tipperary and Waterford, running east and west between the two counties. Formed of Devonian sandstones, the Knockmealdowns have seven peaks with elevations higher than 610 metres (2,000 feet). The highest peak is Knockmealdown, at 795 metres (2,609 feet), in County Waterford.

> **Landmark fact:** During the Irish Famine in the 1840s, the authorities arranged for various building projects to be undertaken in order to provide work. One of those projects was building a wall across the ridge of the Knockmealdown Mountains.
>
> The wall is positioned to mark the boundaries between Tipperary and Waterford. The workers who built this wall were paid a modest sum and many of them died from starvation.

3

LOUGHS AND RIVERS

Water is one of Ireland's most important resources. Our island is surrounded on every side by water, and some counties have a great deal of it; for instance a third of County Fermanagh is composed of water – and most of that is Lower and Upper Lough Erne.

Inland water was very important to the ancient people of Ireland. They believed that water was the route to the 'other world'. Ireland is full of lakes and rivers, each of them with their own unique legends attached. Ireland boasts its fair share of water deities, among them *Boann* (Goddess of the River Boyne) and *Sinnan* (Goddess of the River Shannon).

The Irish word for lake is 'lough' – pronounced *loch* – and there are more than 12,000 loughs in Ireland. Lough Neagh is the largest freshwater lake in Ireland, while the Shannon is the longest river, and while these continue to dominate public attention, there are many others that are aesthetically pleasing to the physical landscape throughout Ireland.

LOUGHS

Lough Neagh (Loch nEachach)

The largest freshwater lake in Ireland, Lough Neagh is situated in mid-Ulster, with five counties touching its shores. It covers an area of 400 square kilometres (154 square miles); it is approximately 32 kilometres (20 miles) long and 14.5 kilometres (9 miles) wide. It was formed by the melting of glaciers at the end of the last Ice Age (around 20,000 years ago). Six major rivers flow into the lough, but only one leaves it – the Lower River Bann.

The name means the lake of the horse-god *Eochu*. He was the lord of the underworld, who was supposed to exist beneath its waters.

Lough Neagh has several local, national and international environmental designations. It was designated as a Ramsar site (wetland sites of international importance) in 1976 because of the very large numbers of wintering wildfowl.

There are several main landmark attractions situated around the shores of the Lough. The archaeological heritage associated with Lough Neagh is considerable and includes Ardboe Cross (see Chapter 5).

A popular story recounts how the famous warrior Fionn Mac Cumhaill caused the creation of Lough Neagh. Legend has it that Fionn was chasing a Scottish giant across Ulster when he picked up a large piece of ground and hurled it at the giant. It overshot and fell into the Irish Sea forming the Isle of Man while the massive crater left behind became filled with water and formed Lough Neagh.

Landmark fact: The name Lough Neagh has survived, despite attempts to change the name of the lough to Lough Sydney and Lough Chichester during the Plantation period.

*Lough Erne (*Loch Éirne*)*

Lough Erne is the name of two connected lakes in County Fermanagh. It is the second largest lake system in Ulster, and the fourth largest in Ireland at 29 kilometres (18 miles) long and 8 kilometres (5 miles) wide. The lakes are widened sections of the River Erne, which flows north and then curves west into the Atlantic. The town of Enniskillen lies on the short stretch of river between the lakes.

The smaller southern lake is called the Upper Lough (as it is further up the river); while the larger northern lake is called the Lower Lough.

Lough Erne was named after Érainn, who was drowned when the lough first burst into existence. In ancient Irish mythology and folklore, Érainn was the favourite maiden of Medb, Queen of Connacht.

One legend suggests that Érainn and her maidens were frightened away from Ráth Cruachan, the traditional capital of Connacht, when a fearsome giant emerged from the cave of Oweynagat. They fled northwards and drowned in a river or lake, their bodies dissolving to become Lough Erne.

While there are more than 150 islands in Lough Erne, one of the most interesting islands is Devenish, where a twelfth-century round tower stands (see Chapter 5). The island was on an old pilgrim route to Croagh Patrick and St Molaise founded a monastic settlement here in the sixth century. Boa Island is the largest island on the lake and is joined to the mainland by a number of bridges.

Boa Island Stone Figures, Fermanagh

Boa Island is on the north shore of Lough Erne, and standing back to back to each other in Caldragh cemetery on the island are two unique stone carvings representing pagan idols. They both have pear-shaped heads, and the larger of these stands 72.5 centimetres (28.5 inches) high. It is thought to represent a Celtic deity and could represent a Celtic goddess as readily as a god, especially given the name of the island.

In Celtic culture, heads were very important because they were thought to contain a person's spirit after their death. Severed heads were taken in triumph after battles. The smaller figure, which is known as 'the Lustyman' because it was found on the nearby island Lusty Mór (moved here in 1939), may in fact be a female figure.

The faces are large with bulging eyes, an open mouth with protruding tongue. The heads are large with the limbs crossed in front of the body. These are usually taken to represent arms, although some suggest that one side is arms and the other side are legs as the end of one limb could be a foot.

Landmark fact: Boa Island is named after Badhbh, sometimes spelled Badb, the Celtic goddess of war. She is one of a triad of Celtic war goddesses that included her sisters, Macha and Morrigan. They were mentioned in Old Irish texts as members of the Tuatha Dé Danann.

*Lough Ree (*Loch na Rí*)*

Lough Ree stretches almost 30 kilometres (18.6 miles) from Lanesborough in County Longford to Athlone in County Westmeath and lays claim to the geographical centre of Ireland. Meaning 'Lake of the Kings', it is the second largest lake on the River Shannon after Lough Derg.

Of special interest are the islands of Lough Ree. The island of Inchcleraun (*Inis Cloithreann*) in the northern part of the lake is the site, according to Irish legend, where the great Queen Medbh met her death.

Inis Cloithreann is derived from Clothru, who was murdered by Medbh so she could rule Connacht from the island. However, Medbh was killed when Clothru's son Furbaide hurled a piece of cheese from his sling that entered Medbh's forehead and struck her dead while she was bathing, thus avenging the murder of his mother.

It is also the site of a monastic settlement founded in AD 540, in the early-Christian era, by St Diarmaid and contains the remains of several ancient churches which still stand on the island. St Diarmaid (or Dermot) was the teacher of St Ciaran, founder of Ireland's famous Clonmacnoise Monastery (see Chapter 8).

This settlement was a place of learning and pilgrimage for centuries and contains the ruins of six churches, graveyards and a fort for protection against Viking raids. The smallest church on the island is called Templedermot, the largest being Templemurray.

There are other islands in Lough Ree that have monastic sites. Many of these still contain ancient ruins from the early Middle Ages. *Inis Inchturk, Inis Inchbofin*, and *Inis Ainghin* are the names of some of the larger ones.

The Lough Ree Monster

Lough Ree is home to one of the most credible lough monster sightings in the world. On 28 May 1960, three priests were enjoying a day's fishing on the lough when one of them noticed an unusual creature about 91 metres (100 yards) away.

The priests then focused on the creature and began to note its size and features in great detail. The story was recorded in many of the local newspapers and made it onto the international stage when the British Broadcasting Corporation (BBC) picked it up.

The report says the monster was 1.8 metres (6 feet) in length and had a head of about 45 centimetres (18 inches) in diameter. Since 1960 there have been a few other sightings by locals and fishermen, and at one stage a reward of £100 was offered to anyone who found the monster dead or alive.

Landmark fact: Lough Ree is the only lough in Ireland where draft netting for trout still continues.

Lough Derg (Loch Derg)

There are at least two Lough Dergs in Ireland, with 'Derg' referring to the colour red in Irish.

The more northerly Lough Derg is located in County Donegal and has been receiving pilgrims for over 1,000 years. While it has forty-six different islands, Station Island and Saints Island are the two largest. Station Island has long served as a retreat for Catholics to reinvigorate their faith.

According to legend, St Patrick spent forty days and nights fasting in a cave on the island. Pilgrimage prayers on Lough Derg have had a pattern of continuity since the 1600s when a Franciscan Friar, Micheál Ó Cléirigh detailed the prayers to be said and the exercises to be performed. It continues to thrive as a strong centre for pilgrimage, with the participants in the three-day retreats going without sleep or food (except for black tea and toast) and walking barefoot over rocks, praying the Stations of the Cross.

Lough Derg has inspired many Irish writers, including Patrick Kavanagh and Nobel Prize-winning poet Seamus Heaney, whose book *Station Island* contains a number of poems dealing with the mystique surrounding the ritual.

Communal prayer on Lough Derg is held in St Patrick's Basilica on Station Island. It is a huge building that took four years to complete and was designated a basilica in 1931. It has thirteen stained glass windows designed by the celebrated Dublin artist Harry Clarke, and each window represents a Station of the Cross. Within each window, Our Lady, St Paul and each of the twelve Apostles are shown holding one of the moments of the Lord's last journey.

The full Irish name for the 'southern' Lough Derg is *Loch Derg Dherc*, meaning 'the Lake of the Red Eye'. This refers to the story of an ancient one-eyed poet, Aitherne, who after having his second eye plucked out by the king, reddened the lake's waters with his blood.

It is a long, narrow freshwater lake in the Shannon River Basin, and is the third largest on the island of Ireland (after Lough Neagh and Lough Corrib). Lough Derg, covers an area of 12,950 hectares (32,000 acres), with shores in Counties Clare (south-west), Galway (north-west), and Tipperary (to the east).

There are a number of islands on Lough Derg, with Illaunmore being the largest. Portumna Castle (see Chapter 5) is located on the north shore of the lough and was built in 1616 by the Governor of Galway, Richard Burke.

Landmark fact: Close downstream from where Lough Derg empties into the Shannon is the location of the hydroelectric power station at Ardnacrusha, which, when built in 1927, was the world's largest.

Lough Corrib (Loch Coirib)

Lough Corrib is the second largest lough in the island of Ireland. It covers 176 square kilometres (68 square miles) and lies mostly in County Galway, with a small area of its north-east corner in County Mayo.

Lough Corrib drains via the Corrib River through Galway city into Galway Bay. The main rivers flowing into Lough Corrib include the River Clare and the canal through the village of Cong, which joins Lough Mask to Lough Corrib.

The name *Loch Coirib* is derived from *Oirbsean*. According to mythology, this refers to the Tuatha Dé Danann figure Manannán mac Lir – a god of the sea.

Islands

Lough Corrib is reputed to have hundreds of small islands, arguably the most famous of which is Inchagoill Island. Located midway between Cong and Oughterard, it is one of the largest of the many wooded islands along Lough Corrib.

This island has spectacular views of the Maumturk range of mountains (see Chapter 2), Joyce country and the mountains of Connemara. It is also home to two ancient venerated sites, set close together in woods – St Patrick's Church, believed to have been erected in the fifth century, and the smaller twelfth-century Church of the Saints.

> **Landmark fact:** The first canal on the island of Ireland was cut in the twelfth century. Known as the Friar's Cut, it allowed boats to pass from Lough Corrib to the sea at Galway.

*Lough Mask (*Loch Measca*)*

Lough Mask is a limestone lough of 83 square kilometres (32 square miles), north of the village of Cong in County Mayo. Lough Mask is the middle of the three lakes that empty into the River Corrib and flow through Galway city, into Galway Bay.

Lough Carra flows into Lough Mask, which feeds into Lough Corrib through an underground stream that becomes the River Cong. Lough Mask is the sixth largest lake, by area, in Ireland.

The island of Inishmaan in Lough Mask contains the remains of a Celtic church of St Cormac, built in the sixth century and enlarged in the twelfth century.

The lough was the scene of the 1882 'Lough Mask murders', when two bailiffs working for Lord Ardilaun were killed. Tensions had risen in the area during the Land War and the proximity of land managed by Charles Boycott. The controversial lack of credible witnesses led to four well-publicised trials of the accused in 1882–83.

According to local legend, a banshee haunts Bly Island, a small island in the lough. There have also been rumoured sightings of a banshee around the shore of the lough as well as other forms of paranormal activity.

Lough Gur

Lough Gur is a small, horseshoe-shaped lake at the base of Knockadoon Hill and has been a regarded as a sacred lake for millennia, going back to the Neolithic period. Throughout the prehistoric era, Lough Gur appeared as an unbroken ring of water, over 8 kilometres (5 miles) in circumference.

Oral tradition strongly associates Lough Gur with the sun goddess Áine. The remains of a crannóg can be seen in the lake, and the ruins of two Desmond Islands are visible on the shore. The island near the eastern shore is named Garrett Island after the 3rd Earl of Desmond, Gerald (or Garrett) Fitzgerald.

In the nineteenth century, Lough Gur was believed to disappear by magic once every seven years. In 1879, a supernatural tree was revealed, growing from the bottom of the lough. Another landmark associated with Lough Gur is the Grange Stone Circle, located on the west of the lake. Measuring nearly 50 metres (164 feet), it is a ring of 113 stones. The entrance is marked with the tallest stones and aligned with the sun in the summer solstice. A heritage centre located by the lakefront in Lough Gur was fully refurbished and restored in 2013. The exhibition within the centre provides an overview of one of Ireland's most important archaeological sites.

The Killarney Lakes (Lochanna Cill Airne)

Arguably the most famous group of lakes in Ireland, the Killarney Lakes consist of the Upper Lake, Lough Muckross (middle lake) and Lough Leane (lower lake).

All three lakes are located in the Killarney National Park (see Chapter 4). Lough Leane is closest to the town of Killarney, and is the largest of the three lakes at 8 kilometres (five miles) long and 4.8 kilometres (3 miles) wide. It has over thirty islands. Lough Muckross is the deepest of the three lakes with a maximum depth of 76 metres (250 feet), while the upper lake, being the smallest in area, has eight large islands.

Inisfallen Island

This 8.5-hectare (21-acre) island is approximately 1.5 kilometres (1 mile) from the shore at Ross Castle. Nothing remains of the seventh-century monastery founded by St Finian the Leper, although it is thought that this monastery gave rise to the name Lough Leane, which means 'Lake of Learning', and it is said that the eleventh-century High King Brian Boru studied on the island.

RIVERS

Ireland's rivers have had a strategic importance since ancient times. They have been used as a means of transport as well as being boundaries between kingdoms – or nowadays, counties. The importance of Uisneach (see Chapter 2) should not be underestimated in the origins of the Irish river system.

One legend tells of how there was a great hailstorm at Uisneach on the occasion of the inauguration of Diarmaid, son of Cerball, as king. Such was its greatness, it was said, that the one shower left twelve chief streams in Ireland forever. A later version of the story attributes the twelve rivers emanating from Uisneach to St Ciarán, who worked a miracle to break a prolonged drought.

Here are some examples, with mention of the landmarks associated with them:

River Shannon (Abhainn na Sionainne)

At 15,532 square kilometres (40,226 square miles) the mighty River Shannon covers a total area of 18.5 per cent of the island of Ireland, and is named after Sionnán, the goddess who was the granddaughter of Manannán mac Lir, god of the sea.

The River Shannon flows south and west from County Cavan to County Limerick along some 286 kilometres (240 miles) of gentle waterway. The Shannon divides the west of Ireland (principally the province of Connacht) from the east and south (Leinster and most of Munster). County Clare, being west of the Shannon but part of the province of Munster, is the major exception.

The source of the Shannon is the Shannon Pot or *Log na Sionna*, a 15-metre (50-foot) wide pool near the Cuilcagh Mountain in west County Cavan. The word log translates as a 'hollow' but can also have an extended meaning as 'the place', indicating a site of great importance.

Sionnán visited the Shannon Pot to eat the fruit of the forbidden 'Tree of Knowledge'. As she began to eat, the waters of the pool overwhelmed her, drawing her down into it to flow out later across the land as the River Shannon.

Famous landmarks situated near the River Shannon include King John's Castle in Limerick (see Chapter 5).

River Bann *(*Bhan Abha*)*

The River Bann is the longest river in Northern Ireland. It rises in the Mourne Mountains and flows into and then out of Lough Neagh. The name derives from 'white river' and there are two sections – Upper Bann and Lower Bann – the total length including its path through Lough Neagh is 160 kilometres (99 miles).

The river's coastal route flows through the holiday resorts of Castlerock, Portstewart and Portrush. The river's oldest surviving bridge is the Bann Bridge at Portadown, built during the seventeenth century.

Famous landmarks situated near the River Bann include Mussenden Temple (see Chapter 1).

The Three Sisters: Barrow, Nore and Suir
River Barrow (*An Bhearú*)

Along with the River Nore and River Suir, the Barrow is one of the Three Sisters. The River Barrow rises at Glenbarrow in the Slieve Bloom Mountains in County Laois. It then flows for 193 kilometres (120 miles) through Counties Laois, Kildare, Carlow, Kilkenny, Wexford and Waterford, before entering the Irish Sea at Waterford Harbour. It is the second longest river in Ireland.

The river is recorded as Berbha in an AD 996 entry in the *Annals of the Four Masters*. Berbha may have been a mythical river goddess. Over 300 years before the Christian era, legend has it that a great battle took place to capture the fort of Dinn Righ, a large mound near Leighlinbridge. The River Barrow is considered one of Ireland's most scenic and picturesque inland waterways.

Famous landmarks situated near the River Barrow include the Browneshill Dolmen near Carlow town (see Chapter 6).

River Suir (*An tSiúr*)

The River Suir, Ireland's third longest river, flows into the Atlantic Ocean near Waterford after a distance of 185 kilometres (115 miles), flowing through towns such as Thurles, Cahir and Clonmel. In the early years of the twenty-first century, the remains of a very large Viking settlement were found at a bend in the river at Woodstown, just upstream from Waterford.

Famous landmarks situated near the River Suir include Cahir Castle (see Chapter 5).

River Nore (*An Fheoir*)

The River Nore rises on the Devil's Bit Mountain in County Tipperary, just over 1.6 kilometres (1 mile) from the source of its sister river, the Suir. It starts out flowing in an easterly direction, passing through Borris-in-Ossory and Castletown. It continues south through Ballyragget, Kilkenny City, Bennettsbridge and Thomastown before joining up with the River Barrow, just upstream of New Ross, at a total of 140 kilometres (87 miles).

Famous landmarks situated along the River Nore include Kilkenny Castle (see Chapter 5).

*River Erne (*Abhainn na hÉirne*)*

The River Erne is the second-longest river in Ulster. It rises on the east shoulder of Slieve Glah Mountain south of Cavan in County Cavan and flows 128 kilometres (80 miles) through Lough Gowna, Lough Oughter and Upper and Lower Lough Erne, County Fermanagh, to the sea at Ballyshannon, County Donegal. The town of Enniskillen is mostly situated on an island in the river, between Upper and Lower Lough Erne.

The Shannon Erne Waterway, a 63-kilometre (39-mile) long canal linking the River Shannon with the River Erne, begins at Leitrim village, which is almost midway between Lough Allen and Carrick-on-Shannon.

Among the famous landmarks situated close to the River Erne are Devenish Round Tower (see Chapter 5).

River Blackwater

While there are a number of lakes named 'Lough Derg', the same applies to the River Blackwater. *An Abhainn Mhór*, also known as the Munster Blackwater, rises in the uplands between Counties Cork and Kerry and flows towards County Waterford, on its way passing through pasture and woodlands.

In total, the Blackwater is 169 kilometres (105 miles) long, and is the larger of the two rivers that share the name. The Munster Blackwater is notable for being one of the best salmon fishing rivers in the country.

Famous landmarks situated near the River Blackwater (Munster) include Lismore Castle (see Chapter 5).

The Ulster Blackwater rises just outside the village of Clogher and flows for 80 kilometres (50 miles) through Counties Armagh and Tyrone before entering Lough Neagh at Maghery.

It also flows between Counties Tyrone and Monaghan, intersecting into Monaghan briefly. Its source is to the north of Fivemiletown,

County Tyrone. The Blackwater's length is 91.7 kilometres (57 miles). The River Blackwater was known in ancient Irish as *Cluain-Dabhail*, meaning 'meadow of Dabhal'.

Among the famous landmarks situated along the River Blackwater (Ulster) includes Castle Leslie (see Chapter 5).

River Boyne *(*Boann*)*

The River Boyne and the Boyne Valley region of County Meath is named after Boann, the water goddess, which translates as 'white cow'. The river rises in the Bog of Allen, County Kildare, and flowing north-east through the fertile Boyne Valley, past the towns of Trim, Navan and Slane in County Meath, it flows on into the Irish Sea at Drogheda in County Louth.

The river is 113 kilometres (70 miles) long – and before bridges were built, a special type of boat called a Boyne curragh was developed. The curragh was made from a wooden frame of hazel wands with an ox hide stretched over it. The boat was very light and buoyant but took great skill by the two-person crew to handle it.

The River Boyne is Leinster's main waterway, and the valley it carves through Counties Louth and Meath has a rich history of settlement, with the passage tombs of Newgrange, Knowth and Dowth at Brú na Bóinne.

Other highlights are Trim Castle, Mellifont Abbey – the first Cistercian monastery established in Ireland – and the Hill of Tara, former seat of the High Kings of Ireland.

Battle of the Boyne

The battle was fought on 1 July 1690 at a fordable river bend 6.5 kilometres (4 miles) west of Drogheda. On 6 July William of Orange entered Dublin, where he gave thanks for victory in Christ Church Cathedral.

The Battle of the Boyne is recalled each July in the celebrations of the Orange Order, not on the first day but on 'the Twelfth', (12 July) for eleven days were lost with the change from the Julian to Gregorian calendar in 1752.

CITY RIVERS

While the Shannon flows through Limerick and the Corrib through Galway, here is a look at some of the rivers that flow through other Irish cities.

River Foyle *(An Feabhal)*

A total length of 128 kilometres (80 miles), the River Foyle flows from the confluence of the Rivers Finn and Mourne at the towns of Lifford in County Donegal and Strabane in County Tyrone. From here it flows to the city of Derry, where it discharges into Lough Foyle and, ultimately, into the Atlantic Ocean.

A Foyle landmark: Millennium Bridge (see Chapter 7).

River Liffey *(An Life)*

The River Liffey is 125 kilometres (78 miles) long and flows through the centre of Dublin. Previously named *An Ruirthech*, the Liffey has always played a central role in the identity and culture of Ireland's capital city.

The Liffey rises in the Liffey Head Bog in the Wicklow Mountains and flows through Counties Wicklow, Kildare and Dublin before entering the Irish Sea at its mouth at the midpoint of Dublin Bay.

The earliest stone bridge over the Liffey was the Bridge of Dublin. It was built by the Dominicans in 1428. It survived well into the eighteenth century. When Dublin became important for business in the seventeenth century, four new bridges were added between 1670 and 1684, including Arran Bridge. The first iron bridge was the elegant Ha'penny Bridge built in 1816. The newest bridge is the Samuel Beckett Bridge, opened in December 2009.

A Liffey landmark: Croke Park (see Chapter 7).

River Lee *(An Laoi)*

The Lee rises in the Shehy Mountains that lie on the western border between Cork and Kerry. At certain points along its 90-kilometre (56-mile) course towards the sea the River Lee widens to form both Inchigeela Lake and Lough Mahon and creates an island on which Cork's city centre is built. It enters the sea at Cork Harbour.

A Lee landmark: St FinBarre's Cathedral (see Chapter 8).

River Lagan *(Abhainn an Lagáin)*

The River Lagan (from Irish meaning 'river of the low-lying district') runs 86 kilometres (53.5 miles) from the Slieve Croob Mountain in County Down to Belfast, where it enters Belfast Lough, an inlet of the Irish Sea. The River Lagan forms much of the border between County Antrim and County Down in the east of Ulster.

A Lagan landmark: Belfast City Hall (see Chapter 7).

4

NATIONAL PARKS AND OTHER LANDMARKS

There are six national parks in Ireland and all are protected sites under the care of the Department of Arts, Heritage, Regional, Rural and Gaeltacht Affairs. The first park established in Ireland was the Killarney National Park in 1932. Since then a further five national parks have been opened, with Ballycroy in County Mayo the most recent. These national parks cover a total area of 635 square kilometres (245 square miles) and contain some of the most important landmarks in Ireland.

BALLYCROY NATIONAL PARK, COUNTY MAYO

Ballycroy National Park was established in November 1998. It is Ireland's sixth national park and is located in north-west County Mayo. It comprises of 11,000 hectares (27,181 acres) of Atlantic blanket bog and mountainous terrain, covering a vast uninhabited and unspoilt wilderness dominated by the Nephin Beg mountain range. To the west of the mountains is the Owenduff Bog. This is one of the last intact active blanket bog systems in Ireland and Western Europe and is an important scientific and scenic feature of the national park.

The park also protects a variety of other important habitats and species under the European Union's Habitats and Birds Directive. Greenland white-fronted geese, golden plover, red grouse and otters are just some of the important fauna found within the park. Also located in north Mayo is another notable landmark: Céide Fields.

Céide Fields

The Céide Fields (*Achaidh Chéide*, meaning 'flat topped hill fields') are the oldest known field systems in the world, over five-and-a-half millennia old. It is a unique Neolithic landscape of world importance on the north County Mayo coast, about 8 kilometres (5 miles) north-west of Ballycastle.

The stone-walled fields, extending over thousands of acres are covered by a natural blanket bog with its own unique vegetation and wildlife. The area has been selectively and sensitively excavated by archaeologists since its discovery in the 1930s by a local schoolteacher who was cutting turf for fuel.

> **Landmark fact:** The visitor centre at the access point to the Céide Fields has won several awards, including Ireland's prestigious Gold Medal for architecture. In the centre of the building is a 4,300-year-old Scots Pine tree, excavated from the fields.

BURREN NATIONAL PARK, COUNTY CLARE

The Burren (*Boireann*, meaning 'a stony place') is a plateau of limestone and shale that covers over 258 square kilometres (100 square miles) of north-west County Clare. Burren is an extremely appropriate name considering the lack of soil cover and the extent of exposed limestone pavement. However, it has been referred to in the past as 'fertile rock' due to the mixture of nutrient rich herb and floral species.

And while it is an amazing landscape of rock set among mountains and valleys, close up one can see wild flowers – for example, in summer a variety of orchids bloom. There are over 600 different flowering plants recorded in the Burren region. The Burren is of particular interest to botanists, since it is the only place in the world where Arctic, Mediterranean and alpine species of wildflowers grow side by side in rock fissures.

The Burren is a geologically distinctive landscape – and has been inhabited for over 6,000 years. The Burren landscape was formed from an accumulation of fish bones and seashells when the sea covered this area many millions of years ago.

The Burren National Park is located in the south-eastern corner of the Burren and is approximately 1,500 hectares (3,706 acres) in size. The parkland was bought by the Irish Government for nature conservation and public access.

The highest point in the Burren National Park is Knockanes, at 207 metres (670 feet), which continues as a curving terraced ridge to Mullaghmór to the south. East of this ridge is an area of extensive, low-lying limestone pavement, containing a number of semi-permanent lakes.

Landmark fact: Michael Cusack, the first secretary of the Gaelic Athletic Association and one of its founders, was born in the parish of Carran on the eastern fringe of the Burren in 1847, during the Great Famine.

CONNEMARA NATIONAL PARK, COUNTY GALWAY

Connemara National Park was established and opened to the public in 1980. It covers some 2,957 hectares (7,307 acres), extending over diverse landscapes of bogs, heaths, woodlands, grasslands and part of the majestic Twelve Bens mountain range (Benbaun, Bencullagh, Benbrack and Muckanacht), as described in Chapter 2.

Much of the park originally formed part of the Kylemore Abbey estate.

Kylemore Abbey

Nestled at the base of Druchruach Mountain on the northern shore of Lough Pollacappul, in the heart of the Connemara Mountains, Kylemore Abbey is regarded as one of Ireland's most romantic buildings.

Kylemore is both a castle and an abbey, built by the Henry family over 150 years ago. When Mitchell Henry and his wife Margaret travelled from Manchester to Connemara in the 1850s they fell in love with the region. Mitchell returned and purchased the estate of Kylemore to build a splendid castle as a romantic gift for his wife.

One mile west of the main abbey building is the 2.5-hectare (6-acre) Victorian walled garden, built by Mitchell Henry at the same time as the construction of Kylemore Castle between 1867 and 1871.

This garden was one of the last walled gardens to be built during the Victorian period in Ireland and is the only garden in Ireland that is located in the middle of a bog. The garden was so advanced for the time that it was even compared with Kew Gardens in London.

The abbey was founded for Benedictine nuns who fled Belgium in the First World War. The nuns had prayer and labour as their ethos – *Ora et Labora* – and had been previously based in Ypres for several hundred years. They provided education to Catholic girls – opening an international boarding school and establishing a day school for girls from the locality, until it was forced to close in 2010.

GLENVEAGH NATIONAL PARK, COUNTY DONEGAL

Located in the heart of the Derryveagh Mountains, Glenveagh National Park covers 6,475 hectares (16,000 acres) and was officially opened in 1986. Within the estate is Glenveagh Castle, a stylish nineteenth-century mansion house built of granite, with a four-storey keep.

Glenveagh was purchased by Irish American John George Adair in 1857. The first part of the castle was built during the following decade, with additions being made until 1885.

Noted for the herds of red deer on the estate (this can be attributed to Adair's wife Cornelia who stocked the estate with the animals after Adair died in 1885), another major attraction of Glenveagh are the gardens. They hold a collection of plants from all over the world, which were planted under the advice of leading landscape artists James Russell and Lanning Roper.

Henry Plumer McIlhenny (who was the Curator of Decorative Arts at the Philadelphia Museum in the United States) was the last person to purchase the property, in 1937. He later agreed the sale of the estate for use as a national park to the Office of Public Works (OPW), and shortly before he died in 1986, he bequeathed Glenveagh Castle as a gift to the state.

The Office of Public Works

The Office of Public Works was established in 1831, by an Act of Parliament: An Act for the Extension and Promotion of Public Works in Ireland. It was given the authority for preserving Ireland's national monuments under legislation enacted in 1882 and 1892. The OPW has responsibility for the care of 780 heritage sites in Ireland, including national monuments, historic parks, gardens and buildings.

WICKLOW MOUNTAINS NATIONAL PARK, COUNTY WICKLOW

Wicklow Mountains National Park is situated just south of Dublin. Covering 20,483 hectares (50,615 acres), this park has the distinction of being the largest national park in Ireland. It is also the only one located in the east of the country, and was established in 1991.

Like the five other national parks, Wicklow was established with the aim of protecting the area's wildlife and landscape, while maintaining and improving the area as a recreational resource for visitors. An estimated 1 million visits are made each year to this park.

This park extends over much of the Wicklow Mountains (Lugnaquilla being the highest in the range at 925 metres (3,035 feet). Upland blanket bog and heath cover the upland slopes and rounded peaks. The wide open vistas are interrupted only by forestry plantations and narrow winding mountain roads. Given this background, the conservation of biodiversity and landscape is considered crucially important here.

Glendalough

Glendalough (see Chapter 8) is one of the best-known areas of the Wicklow Mountains National Park, and the core area of the park surrounds it. It is here that the early medieval monastic settlement of St Kevin is located, dating from the sixth century. The Upper and Lower Lakes of Glendalough give the area its name. From the Irish *Gleann Dá Loch*, it means 'The valley of the two lakes', and the Upper Lake is the larger and deeper of the two.

KILLARNEY NATIONAL PARK, COUNTY KERRY

South and west of the town of Killarney in County Kerry is an expanse of rugged mountainous country. This includes the MacGillycuddy's Reeks (see Chapter 2), the highest mountain range in Ireland, which rises to a height of over 1,000 metres (3,280 feet).

At the foot of these mountains nestles the world famous Lakes of Killarney. The mountains sweep down to the lake shores, their lower slopes covered in woodlands, and it is here that the 10,520-hectare (26,000-acre) Killarney National Park is located.

The park was established in 1932 after the Muckross Estate was donated to the Irish State by Arthur Rose Vincent (following the death of his wife Maud) to protect one of Ireland's most precious natural habitats. It encompasses the three Lakes of Killarney and the mountains and woods surrounding them.

Some of the most impressive archaeological remains in the park are from the early- Christian period. The most important of these features is Inisfallen Abbey, the ruins of a monastic settlement on Inisfallen Island in Lough Leane. It was founded in the seventh century by St Finian the Leper and was occupied until the fourteenth century. *The Annals of Inisfallen*, a record of the early history of Ireland as it was known by the ancient monks, was written in the monastery from the eleventh to the thirteenth centuries.

Killarney National Park contains many features of national and international importance, such as the native oakwoods and yew woods, together with an abundance of evergreen trees and shrubs. It was designated as a Biosphere Reserve in 1981 by the United Nations Educational, Scientific and Cultural Organisation (UNESCO), as part of a world network of natural areas which have conservation, research, education and training as major objectives.

> **Landmark fact:** Killarney National Park is one of the very few places in Ireland that has been continuously covered by woodland since the end of the most recent glacial period, approximately 10,000 years ago.

THE NATIONAL TRUST IN NORTHERN IRELAND

The National Trust for Places of Historic Interest or Natural Beauty, known as the National Trust, is a conservation organisation in Northern Ireland, and the largest membership organisation in the United Kingdom.

The trust describes itself as 'a charity that works to preserve and protect historic places and spaces – for ever, for everyone'. The National Trust was founded in 1895 and given statutory powers, starting with the National Trust Act of 1907.

The list of National Trust properties includes the Giant's Causeway (see Chapter 1) and Florence Court House, one of the most important

Georgian Houses in Ireland, which holds a fascinating collection of Irish furniture and some of the best Rococo plasterwork in Ireland.

AN TAISCE IN THE REPUBLIC OF IRELAND

The National Trust for the Republic of Ireland is known as '*An Taisce*', meaning 'the treasury', and was established in June 1948. It is dedicated to promoting the conservation of Ireland's nature and biodiversity, as well as its built heritage. Naturalist Robert Lloyd Praeger was its first president. *An Taisce* owns a range of Irish heritage properties in trust, including historic buildings and nature reserves.

CORLICAN GRAVEYARD, COUNTY WEXFORD

Corlican is a unique landmark in that it is both a ringfort and a Quaker burial ground. It links early Gaelic settlement, the Cromwellian period and the arrival of the Religious Society of Friends (the Quakers).

Corlican ringfort was constructed in the early medieval period between the early seventh and the late ninth centuries. It is 34 metres (111.5 feet) in diameter and has a roughly circular ditch, a crude rampart and a causeway.

Three Cromwellian soldiers, Robert Cuppage, Thomas Holme and Francis Randall returned to found the Society of Friends in County Wexford. The Quakers later adapted the ringfort by adding a wall, gate and sentinel tree to create a burial ground. The first internment took place in 1659 and burials continued on this site until 1953.

STATELY HOMES

Castletown, County Kildare

Located in the village of Celbridge in County Kildare, this is the largest and most palatial eighteenth-century house in Ireland, and was designed for William Conolly (the Speaker of the Irish House of Commons between 1715 to 1729), by the Florentine architect Alessandro Galilei and Irish architect Sir Edward Lovett Pearce.

Before work commenced on this majestic mansion, Conolly instructed that only Irish materials were to be used in every part of the building. Construction of the mansion began in 1722 and the main

part of the construction was completed by 1729, although the grand staircase was not installed until 1759–60.

Unfortunately Conolly did not get to enjoy his new house, as he died in 1729. Castletown contains 100 rooms and is set in 48.5 hectares (120 acres) of beautiful landscaped grounds. Notable features include the Long Gallery, a 24-metre (79-foot) room on the first floor that was used to entertain guests.

The house remained in the hands of the Conolly family until 1965 when the house was purchased by a property developer, Major Wilson. Fortunately the house was saved in 1967 when along with the demesne lands it was purchased by Hon. Desmond Guinness, founder of the Irish Georgian Society, for £93,000.

The house was opened to the public in the same year and restoration work began, funded by the Irish Georgian Society and private benefactors. In 1979 care of the house passed to the Castletown Foundation, a charitable trust that was established to own, maintain and continue the restoration of the house.

In 1994 the house – with the exception of the contents – was transferred to State care and it is now managed by the Office of Public Works. The transfer to State ownership has paved the way for a major programme of restoration and conservation work on the house and demesne lands.

Springhill House, County Derry

The Lenox-Conyngham family built this magnificent Plantation-style home in the late seventeenth century, near Moneymore village in south Derry. It was home to ten generations of the family and was originally surrounded by a defensive bawn. Around 1765 two single-storey wings were added and the entrance front was modified to its present arrangement of seven windows across its width.

Nowadays there is a visitor centre, a natural play trail and short walks around the estate, as well as numerous portraits and much furniture to admire, while not forgetting Olivia – one of Ireland's best-documented ghosts.

Visitors to the house have been known to feel extreme temperature drops when they step across the threshold of the master bedroom, known as the Blue Room. The guides who lead the tours around the property have put this down to the ghostly presence that is known to haunt the room.

Muckross House

For many visitors the focal point of the Killarney National Park is Muckross House and gardens. This beautiful Victorian mansion stands close to the shores of Muckross Lake and displays all the necessary furnishings and artefacts of the period.

The house was built for Henry Arthur Herbert and his wife, the watercolourist Mary Balfour Herbert. This was actually the fourth house that successive generations of the Herbert family had occupied at Muckross over a period of almost 200 years.

William Burn, the well-known Scottish architect, was responsible for its design. Building commenced in 1839 and was completed in 1843. One famous visitor to Muckross House was Queen Victoria, who visited Killarney in 1861.

Following its acquisition by the State, Muckross House remained closed for thirty years, before being opened to the public in June 1964. It now serves as the main visitor centre for Killarney National Park.

Fota House, County Cork

Fota (derived from the Irish *Fód te*, meaning 'warm soil') House is a Regency-style country house that occupies a sheltered wooded island in east Cork. It was designed for the Smith-Barry family by Sir Richard Morrison and his son William. The de Barry family came from Wales as part of the Norman invasion of Ireland and the family were granted lands at Fota and elsewhere in 1185.

While Fota House was originally a modest two-storey hunting lodge belonging to the Smith-Barry family, it was decided to turn the lodge into a residence that would reflect the elegant Regency style.

Thus two new wings were added and the interior opened up, resulting in the house having over seventy rooms, ranging in size from the more modest servant rooms to the large and beautifully proportioned principal rooms.

Sold by the last of the family to University College Cork in 1975, the house was restored in 2009 and boasts over seventy rooms, many of which are open to the public. Also on display in the main reception rooms is a fine collection of artwork, described as the most significant of its type outside the National Gallery of Ireland.

Fota's internationally renowned gardens are co-managed by the Irish Heritage Trust and the Office of Public Works.

Swiss Cottage, County Tipperary

This unique period piece landmark is a short distance from Cahir Castle (see Chapter 5). Swiss Cottage was built by Richard Butler, the 1st Earl of Glengall to a design by John Nash in 1810 to provide Butler with a fashionable lodge as a base to enjoy his leisure pursuits, such as hunting and fishing. The cottage boasts a thatched roof and ornate timberwork.

Swiss Cottage, constructed as an architectural toy, was designed specifically to blend with nature. The veranda and balconies, although luxury features, have been fashioned to appear humble with exposed rustic tree trunk pillars.

The Swiss Cottage had fallen into disrepair by the 1980s, but a careful conservation plan was put into place by a number of agencies and private benefactors to ensure that it has been restored to its former glory.

A FEW OTHER LANDMARKS ...

John F. Kennedy Arboretum, County Wexford

John F. Kennedy Arboretum is dedicated to the memory of John Fitzgerald Kennedy, thirty-fifth president of the United States of America, whose ancestors were from County Wexford. It consists of 251 hectares (622 acres) and boasts 4,500 types of trees and shrubs, planted in botanical sequence. There are also 200 forest plots grouped by continent. A road provides access to the 271-metre (890-foot) summit of Slieve Coillte (the hill of the wood) from which there are panoramic views.

The arboretum forms part of the Wexford Emigrant Trail, along with the Kennedy Homestead, the Dunbrody Famine Ship and the Irish Emigration Experience. These three key heritage sites are located on a 24-kilometre (15-mile) trail in the vicinity of New Ross. The Kennedy Homestead in Dunganstown is the birthplace of President John F. Kennedy's great-grandfather Patrick Kennedy, and celebrates the story of five generations of the Kennedy dynasty and is still today farmed by his descendants.

Lough Key Forest Park, County Roscommon

The 800-hectare (1,977-acre) Lough Key Forest Park is located on the southern shore of Lough Key, 3 kilometres (1.7 miles) east of the town of Boyle. It is comprised of vast woodland and numerous islands and is located in an area of great historical interest going back to when it was known as Moylurg and the rulers were the McDermott clan.

They ruled this area until the seventeenth century, when it was granted to the King family from England under the Cromwellian settlement. The King family spent their time between the town of Boyle and Moylurg, which they renamed Rockingham. One of the large mansions they built was called Rockingham House and was built where the Moylurg Tower (built in 1973) now stands.

The famous architect John Nash (who also designed Swiss Cottage as well as many other nineteenth-century landmarks) designed the house in 1809–10. The renowned landscaper John Sutherland was commissioned to lay out the park.

In 1957 the house was destroyed by fire, believed to have started in the upper basement due to an electrical fault. The State took over the land in the 1950s and the remaining walls of the house were demolished in 1971.

This vast estate is predominantly covered by forest and woodland with both broadleaf and conifer trees growing within the park. With its diverse habitats this place is home to many species of wildlife. A wealth of historical and archaeological points of interest can be found throughout the park, including ringforts, a souterrain, fishing pavilion, fairy bridge and wishing chair.

The Dark Hedges, County Antrim

This beautiful tunnel of beech trees on the Bregagh Road near Armoy was planted by the Stuart family in the eighteenth century. It was intended as a landscape feature to impress visitors as they approached the entrance to their Georgian mansion, Gracehill House.

Over the decades, the branches grew over the road and became entangled and intertwined, creating a covered passageway. Two centuries later, the trees remain a magnificent sight and have become one of the most photographed natural phenomena in Ireland. Originally, there were about 150 trees, but time has taken its toll and now only about ninety remain.

The iconic set of trees features as the filming location for the King's Road in the epic television series *Game of Thrones*. This has resulted in the area becoming a tourist hotspot: it is estimated that approximately 10,000 people travelled to the north-east of Ireland during 2015 just to visit the Dark Hedges and the production's other scenes in Belfast.

The task of maintaining the Dark Hedges has not been an easy one. A survey of the trees carried out in 2014 showed some were in much better health than others, and that they were vulnerable in severe weather. In January 2016, three of the Dark Hedges trees were uprooted as Storm Gertrude raged across County Antrim.

Scrabo Tower, County Down

Scrabo Tower is located at the top of Scrabo Hill to the west of Newtownards in County Down and overlooks Strangford Lough. This turreted tower, as it stands today, was built on a volcanic plug 165 metres (540 feet) above sea level and is 38 metres (125 feet) high.

It is visible from most of north Down, was built in 1857 as a memorial to Charles Stewart, 3rd Marquess of Londonderry who was one of the Duke of Wellington's generals during the Napoleonic Wars. He was also the man who held the family seat of Mount Stewart (this National Trust house and gardens is nearby on the shores of Strangford Lough).

The tower underwent remedial works in the 1980s and was opened to the public following restoration. A climb of 122 steps takes visitors to the open viewing level at the top of the tower, which gives spectacular views. The building also houses a permanent exhibition on the countryside and surrounding Scrabo Country Park, which has woodland walks and parkland through Killynether Wood.

Landmark fact: Scrabo Tower overlooks woodlands and disused quarries, where Scrabo stone was dug out and used locally as a building material. Greyabbey Monastery and Belfast's Albert Clock were both built with this material. In the early nineteenth century Scrabo Stone was shipped as far away as New York.

5

CASTLES, TOWER-HOUSES AND ROUND TOWERS

Ireland shares an important history with its English, Scottish and Welsh neighbours. Castles first appeared with the arrival of the Anglo-Normans in the twelfth century, and the earliest stone castle in Ireland was Trim Castle in County Meath, built in 1176 by Hugh de Lacy and his son Walter. During the Plantation of Ulster in the early seventeenth century, many new castles were built; but during Cromwell's campaign others were destroyed – and many of the ruins of today date to that period.

A type of tall, usually square, defensible tower known as a tower-house developed later; and many were built several storeys high. They may have numbered as many as 7,000 by the late Middle Ages. Most, if not all, would have stood within a walled enclosure, the bawn, which has seldom survived.

Round towers were ecclestiastical bell-towers used as *cloicteach* (a bell house) for thriving settlements. They were also erected to serve as security lookouts and a place of refuge for members of a community, as well as where valuable relics and manuscripts were kept. They were built between the tenth and twelfth centuries next to monasteries or churches, and there are ruins or complete round towers in twenty-eight of Ireland's counties, with some of the more famous ones based in Leinster – such as Clonmacnoise and Glendalough. Most have high-level doorways requiring a ladder for access, and they are normally situated to the west of the principal church, with the doorway of the tower facing the church.

The twelfth-century Romanesque style round towers were the last to be built – although there was a 'revival' of the round tower, and one famous example includes the round tower built above Daniel

O'Connell's tomb in Glasnevin Cemetery, Dublin. Here are some examples of each type of landmark from the four provinces of Ireland:

CASTLES

Connacht
Athenry Castle, County Galway
The area itself is also renowned for the song *The Fields of Athenry*, but it is one of the most notable medieval walled towns surviving in Ireland, owing its foundation to Meiler de Bermingham, who built his castle on the Clareen River between 1234–35.

Located in the centre of Athlone, the oldest part of the castle is the hall-keep. It is a large rectangular building originally containing only a hall at first-floor level and dark storerooms at ground level. Entrance to the castle was by external wooden stairs leading to a decorated doorway in the east wall at first-floor level.

Portumna Castle, County Galway
This castle is located close to the River Shannon and Lough Derg, and has been classified as a 'large rectangular fortified house with square towers at the corners'. Richard de Burgo (Burke) built it in 1618 but it was never lived in by its owner, and it remained the main seat of the de Burgo family until fire destroyed it in 1826.

A tower stands at each corner of the building, and in them one can see firing holes to be used if the castle needed to be defended. There is a fine Renaissance-style doorway in the first floor on the south side, and the castle has a fine view over Lough Derg.

Thoor Ballylee – Yeats' Tower, County Galway
This is a four-storey tower-house located near the town of Gort and built by the de Burgos in the sixteenth century. Thoor originates from the Irish *túr*, meaning tower. It was brought to public attention by the poet W.B. Yeats as he lived in a cottage nearby in the 1920s and restored the tower while maintaining his creativity for writing. A tablet in the wall commemorates this period spent in County Galway:

> *I, the poet William Yeats*
> *With old mill boards and see-green slates*
> *And smithy work from the Gort forge*
> *Restored this tower for my wife George;*

And may these characters remain
When all is ruin once again.

In 1963, the Yeats family placed the property in the hands of a trust in order to ensure its restoration and maintenance. The Nobel Laureate for Literature Seamus Heaney from County Derry described this landmark as the most important building in Ireland.

Rockfleet Castle, County Mayo

Rockfleet Castle is located on an inlet of Clew Bay in County Mayo, close to Achill Island. It is also known as Carraigahowley, derived from the Irish *Carraig an Chabhlaigh*, which translates as 'rock of the fleet'.

This tower-house, built in the mid-sixteenth century, is most famously associated with Granuaile, the chieftain of the O'Malley clan and notorious pirate queen who plundered and raided the coasts from Scotland to the south-west of Ireland in the late sixteenth century.

Rockfleet was owned by Richard *an Iarainn* 'the Iron' Bourke, who inherited it from his Anglo-Norman ancestors. Granuaile married Richard, her second husband, in 1567 (at the age of 16 she had married Dónal *an Chogaidh* (Dónal of the Wars)).

Granuaile spent her latter years here at Rockfleet, and legend has it that the door in the top-most room was where the rope from her galley came through from the outside and was tied to her bed. It is believed that Granuaile died at Rockfleet Castle around 1603.

The castle, restored in the 1950s, is over 18 metres (59 feet) high and has a small rectangular corner turret rising above the parapet. Of the four floors, including ground level, the middle two are of wood and the top one is stone-flagged.

Leinster
Dublin Castle

Viking defences had been established on the site in the tenth century, but the castle dates from King John's first Dublin court of AD 1204, when he ordered Meiler FitzHenry to build a fortress with strong walls and good ditches for the defence of the city and safe custody of treasure. Four centuries later, during the reign of Elizabeth I, this famous landmark became the centre of English government and administration in Ireland rather than a military centre.

The south-east Record Tower is the last intact medieval tower, not only of Dublin Castle, but also of Dublin itself. It functioned as a high-security prison and held native Irish hostages captive in Tudor times.

In the eighteenth century a Georgian palace was constructed. By the following century (the castle continued as the viceroy's seat after the Act of Union in 1801) Dublin Castle was firmly regarded as the symbol of the English Ascendancy in Ireland.

Dublin Castle was handed over to the new Irish State in 1922, and nowadays it is the setting for significant state functions, such as when Britain's Queen Elizabeth visited in 2011.

The Chester Beatty Library is based in the grounds of Dublin Castle and spread over two floors. This remarkable collection includes more than 20,000 manuscripts, rare books and other objects of artistic and historical importance.

Landmark fact: The city of Dublin actually gets its name from the *Dubh Linn*, or Black Pool, on the site of the present Castle Gardens and Coach House.

Kilkenny Castle, County Kilkenny

Originally the site of a monastery set up by St Cainneach, Kilkenny Castle has been an important site since Richard de Clare, the 2nd Earl of Pembroke (who has since in historical terms become commonly known by his nickname Strongbow) who built the first castle on the site, which was completed in the latter years of the twelfth century. This was a square-shaped stone castle with towers at each corner and three of these original four towers survive to this day.

Strategically, it was built to control a fording-point of the River Nore and the junction of several routeways, and formed an important element of the defences of the town of Kilkenny. Badly damaged in the Cromwellian Wars, it was reconstructed and remodelled more than once, the second time in an attempt to restore its medieval character.

The property was transferred to the people of Kilkenny in 1967 for the grand sum of £50 and the castle and grounds are now managed by the Office of Public Works. The central block now includes a library, drawing room and bedrooms, as well as the beautiful Long Gallery.

Trim Castle, County Meath

Trim was founded by the Normans on the banks of the River Boyne, and right in the centre of the town is one of the finest examples of Norman architecture still standing in Ireland today.

Trim Castle, also known as St John's Castle, is the largest Anglo-Norman castle in Ireland, and was built in 1183 by Hugh de Lacy and his son Walter. It was constructed over a thirty-year period. Hugh was granted the Freedom of Meath by King Henry II in 1172 in an attempt to curb the expansionist policies of Richard de Clare, also called 'Strongbow'.

The massive three-storey keep main building, the central stronghold of the castle, was built by William Peppard on the site of an earlier fortress, and was protected by a moat. The main chambers in the keep were used for public gatherings such as feasts.

Trim Castle remained in use until the mid-seventeenth century, when Cromwellian forces occupied it. The castle was partially restored in the last decade of the twentieth century and reopened in 2000 by the Office of Public Works as part of Ireland's Millennium Project.

Slane Castle

The grounds of Slane Castle have been used to host rock concerts since 1981, and musicians who have played at the venue include Bob Dylan and Bruce Springsteen. The castle was built in 1701 by the Conyngham family, and is now owned by Lord Henry Mountcharles, a descendant of that family.

Leap Castle, County Offaly

Leap Castle is said to be the most haunted castle in Ireland. It was built by the O'Bannon clan and was originally called *Léim Uí Bhanáin* (as was the fertile land around the castle which was associated with the Bannon clan) for their rulers, The O'Carrolls, Princes of Ely.

The Bannons built it around 1250. It was erected on a most commanding site facing the Great Pass through the Slieve Bloom Mountains to fortify the valley between the provinces of Leinster and Munster.

The Annals of the Four Masters record that the Earl of Kildare, Gerald FitzGerald, tried unsuccessfully to seize the castle in 1513. Three years later, he attacked the castle again and managed to partially demolish it. However, by 1557 the O'Carrolls had regained possession.

One of the most gruesome murders to take place in Leap Castle occurred in 1532 in a room above the main hall of the castle which is now known as 'the Bloody Chapel', due to a bitter succession dispute which arose over the leadership of the clan. Following the death of Mulroney O'Carroll, a fierce rivalry for the leadership erupted within the family. One of the brothers was a priest. While he was saying Mass for a group of his family, his rival brother burst into the chapel, plunged his sword into him and fatally wounded him. The priest fell across the altar and died in front of his family.

The priest's spirit is said to haunt the Bloody Chapel and is thought to be one of Leap's earliest ghosts. Even centuries later when the castle lay in a state of ruin, passers-by have seen the window of the room light up suddenly late into the night.

Since 1991, Leap Castle has been privately owned, and in recent years, the castle has gained a certain notoriety due to its ghostly reputation. It has been visited by paranormal investigators from various international television companies. Visits to Leap Castle are by appointment only.

Enniscorthy Castle, County Wexford

The castle is sited at the head of the Slaney River in the centre of Enniscorthy. It is a grey stone Norman castle, built during the 1230s by Philip de Prendergast, consisting of four drum towers at the corners and a rectangular keep four storeys tall.

Down the centuries, the castle has been home to Norman knights, English armies, Irish rebels and prisoners, and local merchant families. Enniscorthy Castle became the property of the Crown in the 1530s and was once home to the poet Edmund Spencer. It is believed that the poem *The Faerie Queen*, written by Spencer, was based on Queen Elizabeth. She was said to be so pleased that she chose to grant him a pension for his life and made a gift of the castle to him.

In 1649 the castle was captured by Cromwellian troops after a siege, and in 1798 was used as a prison during the Rising. County Wexford was a centre of conflict during that prominent era in Irish history.

The castle was restored twice in the nineteenth century, once by the Earl of Plymouth and changed into a dwelling and again by a local MP at the end of the century, when it remained a home until 1951. Nowadays, the Wexford County and Folk Museum is located in the castle, and it has an extensive display of items relating to the castle's use as a prison during the Rising of 1798.

Munster
Bunratty Castle, County Clare

Caisleán Bhun Raithe translates as 'the castle at the bottom of the Ratty'. The Ratty River, alongside the castle, flows into the nearby Shannon estuary. The present castle is the third on this site, and is one of the most popular tourist attractions in Ireland.

This castle is a large single tower-house over five floors, built in grey stone. The main block of the castle has three floors over dungeons. It is the most authentically restored and complete medieval fortress in Ireland.

The first stone castle on the site was built by Thomas de Clare in the thirteenth century, but by the mid-fifteenth century Síoda MacConmara had built the castle that stands there today.

Bunratty Castle and its lands were granted to various Plantation families, the last of which was the Studdart family, who left in 1804. Lord Gort purchased it in 1954, and following extensive restoration work with the help of the Office of Public Works, the Irish Tourist Board and Shannon Development, it was then opened to the public in 1962 as a national monument and is open to visitors all year round.

One of the main attractions to visitors of Bunratty Castle is the collection of medieval furniture and objects, with over 450 pieces on display.

> **Landmark fact:** Bunratty Castle was once defended by Admiral Sir William Penn, father of William Penn, the founder of Pennsylvania in the United States.

Blarney Castle, County Cork

Blarney, a castle named after its local area, is laid on very strong foundations. Built in 1446 by Cormac McCarthy, King of Munster, the castle originally dates from before 1200, when a timber house is believed to have been built on the site.

The castle was sold and changed hands a number of times before being purchased in 1703 by Sir James Jefferyes, then governor of Cork city. Blarney Castle is now a partial ruin with some accessible rooms and battlements.

Blarney Castle is arguably most famous for its famous 'stone of eloquence', better known as the Blarney Stone. Legend suggests that kissing this stone is said to bestow great eloquence, or the 'Gift of the Gab'. Tourists visiting Blarney Castle who wish to kiss this famous stone must lean backwards – grasping an iron railing – from the parapet walk. The stone itself is a 1.2-metre by 0.3-metre (4-foot by 1-foot) limestone block set in the battlements 25 metres (83 feet) above the ground.

> **Landmark fact:** The word 'Blarney' was introduced into the English language by Queen Elizabeth I due to her irritation with the lack of effort by the Lord of Blarney – who promised much and delivered little. The queen is said to have eventually cried out 'Blarney, Blarney, what he says he does not mean. It is the usual Blarney.' A new word in the English language was thus created!

Ross Castle, County Kerry

This castle is located on Ross Island on the edge of Lough Leane in Killarney National Park. The date of its foundation is uncertain, but it was probably built in the late fifteenth century by one of the O'Donoghue Ross chieftains.

It is surrounded by a fortified bawn, its curtain walls defended by circular flanking towers, two of which remain. Ross Castle was the last place in Munster to succumb to Cromwell's forces, in 1652. Much of the bawn was removed by the time the barrack building was added on the south side of the castle, sometime in the middle of the eighteenth century.

Ross Castle has been restored in recent times, and is now operated by the Office of Public Works, with a display room on the main floor of the castle.

King John's Castle, County Limerick

King John's Castle sits on King's Island on the banks of the River Shannon in the heart of Limerick city. In 1197 Limerick was given its first charter by King John and its first mayor, Adam Sarvant, a few years after Anglo-Normans established themselves in the area.

A castle, built on the orders of King John and bearing his name, was completed between 1200 and 1212. It was built on the site of an original Viking settlement. By the fourteenth century the city was divided into an area which became known as English Town on King's Island, while another settlement, named Irish Town, had grown up on the south bank of the river. The O'Briens and McNamaras captured it for a period of that century.

The castle went into decline until 1642, and this was exacerbated when it was occupied by people escaping the Confederate Wars and the walls of the castle were badly damaged in the Siege of Limerick. There was also considerable damage caused during the Williamite sieges in the 1690s and so the castle has been repaired and restored on a number of occasions.

King John's Castle is considered to be one of the best preserved Norman castles in Europe, and has kept a large amount of its original features, including a huge gatehouse and its outer walls with castellated corner towers and battlements.

Landmark fact: King John was King of England from April 1199 until his death from dysentery aged 50 in 1216. He was appointed Lord of Ireland at age 12, and is most well known for signing Magna Carta into existence in 1215.

Cahir Castle, County Tipperary

Situated on an islet on the River Suir, the term Cahir derived from *cathair* (stone fort) and it is one of the largest castles in Ireland, built in 1142 by Conor O'Brien, Prince of Thomond, on the site of an earlier native fortification.

In 1375, the castle was granted to James Butler, the newly created Baron of Cahir, for his loyalty to King Edward III. The castle was enlarged and remodelled between the fifteenth and seventeenth centuries, but fell into ruin in the late eighteenth century and was partially restored in the 1840s.

In 1961 the last Lord Cahir died, and the castle reverted to the Irish State. By the late twentieth century the castle was named a national monument, and is now managed by the Office of Public Works. The castle is one of the best preserved standing castles of Ireland. It has retained its impressive keep, tower and much of its original defensive structure from the fourteenth century.

Lismore Castle, County Waterford

Lismore Castle has long been associated with some of the most famous people in Irish, British and American history. Overlooking the Blackwater Valley, there has been a castle at Lismore ever since 1185, when Prince John built on the present site.

When John became King of England he handed the castle over to the Church and it was used as a Bishop's Palace until 1589. The earliest remaining part of the castle is a round tower, which dates back to the thirteenth century.

In 1589, the castle was leased and later bought outright by Sir Walter Raleigh. In 1602, when Raleigh was imprisoned in the Tower of London for high treason, he sold Lismore, along with 16,996 hectares (42,000 acres) for £1,500 to Richard Boyle, who later became the first Earl of Cork. Richard Boyle's youngest son, Robert Boyle, the philosopher and father of modern chemistry, was born at Lismore in 1626.

Three centuries later, Kathleen Kennedy, sister of President John F. Kennedy, spent a lot of time at Lismore. One of her guests was her brother John in 1947, and it was during this visit that he made his way to County Wexford to locate his ancestral home.

Nowadays Lismore Castle is a private residence and there is no public access. However, from March to October the impressive gardens around Lismore Castle are open to the public. Set within the castle walls and comprising 2.8 hectares (7 acres), the gardens have spectacular views of the castle and surrounding countryside.

Ulster
Dunluce Castle, County Antrim

The iconic ruin of Dunluce Castle, situated on the north coast of Antrim, has a long and intriguing history. It is thought that the earliest parts of the castle are possibly fourteenth century, built for the 2nd Earl of Ulster, Richard de Burgh, on the site of an earlier fort dating back to the Vikings, but it is not documented until ownership by the MacQuillan family in the early sixteenth century. In fact, the earliest written record of the castle was in 1513.

Despite the castle now being in a totally ruined state, it still has partial remains of its round corner towers and outer wall. The remains of the castle are connected to the mainland by a modern wooden bridge, and formerly by a drawbridge.

Dunluce was seized by the ambitious MacDonnell clan in the 1550s, led by the famous warrior chieftain Sorley Boy MacDonnell during an era of violence, intrigue and rebellion. In the seventeenth century Dunluce was the seat of the earls of County Antrim and saw the establishment of a small town in 1608.

As for the place name Dunluce, it is uncertain to what it refers. The first element of the name originates from the Irish word *Dún*, which means a fort, but the second half of the name appears in many guises.

In older Irish language texts, the name is given as either *Dún Lios* or *Dún Libhsi*. *Lios* is another word for an enclosure or fort, which would give the name Dún Lios the inelegant meaning of 'Fort-fort', while all attempts to find a meaning for Libhsi have been unsuccessful.

The castle was badly damaged in an artillery attack by the English deputy Sir John Perrott in 1584; while in 1639, Dunluce Castle paid the penalty for its precarious position when the kitchen, complete with cooks and dinner, fell off the cliff during a storm. The castle decayed from the later seventeenth century onwards, but is now a highlight of the 53-kilometre (33-mile) Causeway Coast Way walking trail.

> **Landmark fact:** The Spanish Armada galleass *La Girona* was wrecked close to the castle in 1588. A few of its recovered canons allegedly were installed at the castle. Some of its cargo was successfully salvaged in the 1960s, and is now displayed in the Ulster Museum in Belfast.

Carrickfergus Castle

Situated in the town of Carrickfergus, the castle has wonderful views over Belfast Lough. It was probably constructed by John de Courcy in the years following his initial conquest of Ulster in 1177, and was used as his headquarters until 1204, when de Courcy lost the castle to Hugh de Lacy (son of de Lacy who built Trim Castle).

When King John came to Ireland in 1210, he captured the castle. Almost five centuries later Frederick Schomberg, 1st Duke of Schomberg, did the same, on this occasion on behalf of King William. The Napoleonic Wars in 1797 saw the castle being used as a prison as well as an armoury. During the First World War and Second World War the castle was used as a garrison and an air raid shelter.

In 1928, Carrickfergus Castle was declared a national monument and opened to the public. Its core, and oldest part, is the inner ward and four-storey keep that is now used for historical displays. The castle also has the remains of its original curtain wall, along with a postern gate on the seaward side and an eastern tower.

Landmark fact: An excavation of the Carrickfergus Castle site in 2015 led by experts from Queen's University Belfast and the Northern Ireland Environment Agency, discovered parts of a nineteenth-century tunnel extending into the area where the medieval Great Hall once stood.

Doe Castle, County Donegal

Doe Castle is located about 1.6 kilometres (1 mile) from the Carrigart to Creeslough road. The castle is on an inlet of Sheephaven Bay, protected by sea on three sides, and by a moat cut into the rock on the landward side.

The name Doe originates from *tuath*, the Irish word for territory. This impressive fortified castle has a central tower, battlements and a defensive wall enclosing a courtyard. The central tower is 15 metres (50 feet) high, with a large room on each of the four levels.

Doe Castle was built in the sixteenth century and was a stronghold of Clan Suibhne (MacSweeney), who became known as *MacSuibhne na dTuath* – MacSweeney of the Territory.

Owen Roe O'Neill led the Irish Confederates from Doe Castle in 1642 in the Wars of the Three Kingdoms. During the seventeenth century the castle changed hands a number of times, and was taken by the English.

Abandoned around 1700, it fell into ruin before being restored as a residence by George Vaughan Hart in 1810. He made his home there until 1864 and left his initials (G.V.H.) embedded on the wall above the door of the eastern entrance. The last occupant was a Church of Ireland minister, and after his departure the castle fell into disrepair.

In 1932 the Irish Land Commission (Office of Public Works) bought the castle and vested it as a national monument.

Donegal Castle, County Donegal

Donegal Castle dominates the centre of Donegal town on the bend of the River Eske. The castle was initially built as a stronghold by the chieftain Hugh O'Donnell in 1474 for the O'Donnell clan.

The O'Donnells left Ireland in 1607, joining the Flight of the Earls, but before they left they tried to destroy the castle to prevent it being used by the English against other Gaelic clans. Sir Basil Brooke was granted the castle and its land in 1610, and quickly restored and improved it.

He made additions in a Jacobean style, adding a large manor house wing in the keep, a gable, additional windows and a fortified tower. The castle stayed in the Brooke family for generations until it fell into disrepair in the eighteenth century after Cromwell's invasion. In the late 1990s the tower-house was totally restored, leaving the remaining wings as ruins. Donegal Castle is now maintained by the Office of Public Works.

Dundrum Castle, County Down

One of the finest Norman castles in Ireland, with views to the sea and the Mourne Mountains. Dundrum Castle was founded in 1177 by John de Courcy, following his invasion of Ulster. This medieval coastal castle, with circular keep and massive walls, stands on the top of a rocky hill commanding fine views south over Dundrum Bay and the Mourne Mountains.

Its purpose was to guard the land routes from Drogheda via Greencastle to Downpatrick. It was captured by King John in 1210, who spent money for minor works to the castle and paid for a garrison there. Subsequently the castle passed to the Earls of Ulster in 1227 and, from the middle of the fourteenth century, was in the hands of the Irish Magennises of Mourne.

Castle Leslie, County Monaghan

Castle Leslie Estate, home to an Irish branch of the Scottish clan Leslie is located on a large estate of land adjacent to the village of Glaslough in County Monaghan.

In 1665 Glaslough Castle and demesne was sold by Sir Thomas Ridgeway to the Bishop of Clogher, John Leslie. The bishop died at the age of 100 in 1671 and the original deed to the castle is still in the family archives.

The current castle is fashioned in the Scottish Baronial style and was designed by the firm of Lanyon, Lynn and Lanyon in 1870 for Sir John Leslie, 1st Baronet, MP. It is situated where the earlier castle stood and never had a defensive purpose. Nowadays the castle and estate is used for equestrian events, a cookery school, banqueting and other events.

ROUND TOWERS

Here is a look at a number of round towers from each of the four Irish provinces:

Ulster
Antrim, County Antrim
The tower was built in either the tenth or eleventh century and is known locally as 'The Steeple' and is based in a small area of parkland, enclosed by mature trees in Antrim town. It is 28 metres (92 feet) tall, and has some irregularities in its conical cap, due to it being struck by lightning in 1819.

It has one unique feature: a ringed cross, carved in relief on a stone above the lintel of the doorway on the north-eastern portion of the tower. A small plaque with a neoclassical frame is set on the external wall, but no inscription is now visible.

Drumlane Abbey and Round Tower, County Cavan
The imposing Drumlane Round Tower forms part of an ancient monastic site located just south of Milltown, County Cavan, in a wonderful setting close to Garfinny Lough. Along with an abbey and a church, the distinguished round tower was founded by St Columba in AD 555.

During the Middle Ages, the Drumlane estate was ruled by the O'Farrelly clan. The nearby church is part of an abbey founded here by monks from Kells in County Meath.

The earliest parts of the building are thirteenth century, but it was substantially altered in the fifteenth century, the period from which the carved heads outside the doorways and windows date.

The round tower is the most distinguished part of the estate, a tall circular stone structure that remains the only surviving round tower in the diocese of Kilmore.

Landmark fact: The original round tower at Drumlane was made of wood but it was replaced with stone in the twelfth century under the supervision of Augustinian monks.

Devenish Island and Round Tower, County Fermanagh

Founded by St Molaise in the sixth century, this monastic site was built on a pilgrimage route to Croagh Patrick in County Mayo. During its history it has been raided by Vikings (AD 837), burned (AD 1157) and flourished (during the Middle Ages) as a parish church site and as St Mary's Augustine Priory. The priory has a fine Gothic sacristy door decorated with birds and vines.

Devenish continued to be an important religious centre up until the beginning of the seventeenth century. The 25-metre (82-foot) tall round tower originated in the twelfth century, while a beautiful, intricately carved stone high cross from the fifteenth century is nearby.

The tower has wooden floors and can be climbed by the public via a series of ladders. The doorway is the customary 3 metres (10 feet) above ground level. But perhaps the most unusual feature is a beaded cornice running around the top of tower with a head sculpture featured above the bell-storey windows.

Landmark fact: An early eleventh-century book shrine known as the *Soiscel Molaise* that has links to Devenish Island is now kept in the National Museum in Dublin.

Leinster
Clonmacnoise, County Offaly

Clonmacnoise is a landmark site at the crossroads of Ireland where the waterway of the River Shannon – flowing north to south – meets the Slige Mór, one of the east–west trackways of ancient Ireland.

There are two round towers at the site of Clonmacnoise: O'Rourke's Tower and *Teampaill Finghin*, or McCarthy's Tower. The former is situated in the north-west corner of the old graveyard. According to the *Annals of the Four Masters*, it was built by Turlough O'Connor and O'Malone, and completed in 1124. It was damaged by lightning in 1135 and the tower is both topless and altered. The tower is thought to be missing slightly more than a third of its true height.

Teampaill Finghin is often called the second round tower of Clonmacnoise, and it is 16.7 metres high (55 feet) with a diameter of almost 4 metres (13 feet) at the base. It is one of only two surviving examples of an intact engaged round tower. The conical cap, with its unusual herringbone pattern, the only function of which is decorative, was taken down and reset by the Office of Public Works in 1879.

Glendalough, County Wicklow

The famous round tower at Glendalough forms part of an important complex of Irish ecclesiastical settlement, known as the 'seven churches of Glendalough', and the first Christian monastery was established there by St Kevin. There are three towers at Glendalough, with the largest considered by many to be one of the most finely constructed and beautiful round towers in Ireland.

Situated in a forested valley, the 30.48 metre (100 feet) tall tower's conical roof was rebuilt in 1876, using the original stones that were found inside the tower. The round tower is divided internally into six storeys by timber floors, connected by ladders.

Clondalkin, County Dublin

This is the only complete round tower in the Dublin area, and is situated in the centre of Clondalkin village. Built on the site of a monastery founded by St Mochua in the seventh century, the tower stands at 27.5 metres (90 feet) high and is thought to be an early example of a round tower, as the granite on the lintels is flat.

A most unusual feature of this tower is the very pronounced buttress at the base. It is constructed from a different variety of stone to the main tower, which may suggest that it was added later, perhaps at some point in the nineteenth century. There are six windows in the tower, of which the four highest face north, south, west and east.

Landmark fact: The local GAA club in Clondalkin is named in honour of the round tower.

Kilree Round Tower, County Kilkenny

This well-preserved 29-metre (96-foot) high round tower is located about 4 kilometres (2.5 miles) south-east of the village of Kells. It is missing its original conical top and is perched on the circular boundary wall of a churchyard, dominating this old monastic site. Near it stands the ruined church with flat-headed doorway and antae. The tower doorway faces the church ruin.

There is a sandstone high cross across the field to the west of the tower. It is said to be of ninth-century origin, and although it is badly weathered, it is still beautifully carved with bosses, ornament, interlace and what were once some figure carvings.

Connacht
Kilmacduagh, County Galway

Kilmacduagh is the tallest round tower in Ireland at 33.5 metres (110 feet). It is located 8 kilometres (5 miles) south-west of the town of Gort and has a number of very distinctive features.

There are eleven angle-headed windows in the tower, some of which have been restored. The most obvious feature of the tower is its tilted nature, towards the south-west. The seventh-century St Colman, son of Duagh, established a monastery on land given to him by his cousin King Guaire, making this one of Ireland's older monastic sites. Kilmacduagh Round Tower has often been compared to another famous landmark – the Leaning Tower of Pisa in Italy.

Killala, County Mayo

This is a complete round tower located in the centre of Killala – a town in north County Mayo that witnessed the first battle of the French force of General Humbert in the 1798 Rebellion, which landed at nearby Kilcummin Harbour.

The Killala Round Tower is 25.5 metres (84 feet) high, standing on a 1-metre (3-foot) high plinth, with a doorway 3.3 metres (11 feet) above the ground. Some say that the souterrain in the grounds of the church across the road leads into it.

The original monastic foundation dates from the time of St Patrick, who placed his disciple St Muiredach in charge of the church. In a well that still flows close to the town, beside the sea, it is reputed that St Patrick baptised 12,000 converts in a single day.

Munster
Cloyne, County Cork

The round tower in the town of Cloyne in east County Cork stands between Georgian houses on Church Street in the centre of the town, and was originally part of an ecclesiastical site. The monastery was founded by St Colman Mac Lénine in AD 560.

Cloyne is a well-preserved round tower but lacking its cap. On 10 January 1749 a lightning storm caused notable damage. However drawings prove that the conical cap on the tower had been replaced by battlements before that time.

Built on a network of caves which are all but impassable, it is rumoured that in the penal days (late seventeenth century) priests used a secret underground link from Cloyne House to the Catholic graveyard in order to say Mass for the people.

Roscrea, County Tipperary

Another round tower situated in a town centre is in Roscrea, with its capless limestone tower. St Cronan founded a monastic site here in the late sixth century, the remains of which are now divided by the main road through the town.

A safe haven was particularly needed in Roscrea during the ninth and tenth centuries, as Viking raids on affluent monasteries were a frequent threat. The tower as it is today measures 18 metres (60 feet), but it originally rose to a height of 24 metres (80 feet).

The earliest record of the tower states that it was struck by lightning in 1131, and the top was removed following an incident in the town in 1798, when the top floor was used by an insurgent sniper, who availed of the prime position it offered to fire at sentries in the barracks.

Landmark fact: Up until the new Church of Ireland church was constructed in 1812, the round tower acted as a belfry.

Ardmore, County Waterford

This tower stands in a churchyard on a hill overlooking the village of Ardmore. Its height from ground level to the base of the intact conical top is about 26 metres (85 feet). The Ardmore monastic settlement is thought to have been founded by St Declan in the fifth century.

The round tower may be of twelfth-century origin, but could have been built as early as the tenth century, though the first known mention of the tower is in 1642 when it and a nearby castle were occupied by Irish forces.

Landmark fact: In 1591, Ardmore Cathedral was leased to famous explorer Sir Walter Raleigh, who held it for two years.

6

HISTORIC MONUMENTS: HIGH CROSSES, FORTS AND STONES

From ancient times, the people of Ireland have been proud of the structures that illustrate their beautiful landscape.

Ringforts are the most numerous ancient monument found in Ireland. They are known by a variety of names, including *fort, ráth, dún, lios, cashel* and *caher*. They consist of an area, usually circular, enclosed by one or more earthen banks or, occasionally, by stone walls.

It has been suggested that they were not built to repel sieges designed to annex territories, but rather to repel the lightning cattle raids which were common during the early-Christian period in Ireland.

Hillforts are enclosed sites, usually of several hectares, consisting of one or more banks and ditches surrounding a hilltop, often following the contours of the land. There are at least fifty examples known in Ireland. They are sometimes on sites enclosing earlier burial cairns and are often denoted as royal sites in history and mythology.

The high cross is synonymous with early-Christian Ireland, and they were decorated with pictures which taught biblical stories to the largely illiterate population. There are examples of them in every province in Ireland, and they showed how powerful religious communities (as in Glendalough and Monasterboice) supported and encouraged art in that period of Irish history.

Standing Stones formed a link between prehistoric Ireland and early-Christian times. Some bear inscriptions in the ancient Ogham system, a unique written language used in Ireland. The tallest is the 5.7-metre (19-foot) high monolith at Punchestown, while the Browneshill Dolmen (portal tomb) in County Carlow has the largest capstone in Ireland, and one of the largest in Europe.

Stone circles are a ring of standing stones, usually freestanding, enclosing an open area, sometimes with a grave or burial mound at the centre. They appear to have a ritual function and date to late Neolithic/Early Bronze Age times. Examples include Drombeg in Cork and Beaghmore in Tyrone.

Here is a selection of these historic monuments, arranged by province:

ULSTER

Navan Fort, County Armagh

To the west of Armagh city lies the ancient Navan Fort, known as *Emain Macha*, named after the goddess Macha. It first appears as a rounded hill encircled by a bank of mature trees. At the top of the hill is a large mound, about 5.5 metres (18 feet) high and 45.7 metres (150 feet) across.

In early-Irish mythology, it was the headquarters associated with the Ulster Cycle, particularly King Concobhar MacNessa and his Red Branch Knights, and it was here that the Irish mythical hero Cú Chulainn spent much of his youth before going out to face the army of Queen Medbh advancing from Connacht.

Excavations of the aforementioned large mound at its centre, carried out between 1963 and 1971, showed that a ditched enclosure, some 150 metres (492 feet) in diameter, had been built in the Late Bronze Age.

The Royal Sites of Ireland

The royal sites of ancient Ireland were all sites of major royal inauguration, ceremony and assembly, representing each of the four Irish provinces: Ulster, Leinster, Munster and Connaught, as well as the region of Meath.

Navan Fort is portrayed as the royal site for the Kings of Ulster; Dún Ailinne for the Kings of Leinster; Cashel for the Kings of Munster and Rathcroghan for the Kings of Connaught. Tara was the seat of the Kings of Meath and the seat of the Irish High Kings. In addition the Hill of Uisneach is traditionally the epicentre of Ireland, where the five provinces met. These sites are strongly linked to myth and legend and are associated with the transformation of Ireland from paganism to Christianity by St Patrick.

Kilnasaggart Inscribed Stone, Armagh

Stone sculpture has a long tradition in Irish history, and when monasteries turned to this medium it expressed their Christian faith. Standing at almost 2 metres (6.5 feet) tall, Kilnasaggart, meaning 'the church of the priest', inscribed stone is regarded as being one of the oldest in Ireland, believed to date to around AD 700.

The granite pillar is located in the beautiful Slieve Gullion region, which is rich in historical monuments. The stone stands at the north end of an enclosed area some 15.25 metres (50 feet) in diameter, and has thirteen crosses inscribed on it. The Ogham inscription on the stone translates to 'This place, bequeathed by Termoc, son of Ceran Bic (little), under the patronage of Peter, the Apostle'.

Excavations at the site in 1966 and 1968 revealed an early-Christian graveyard with graves oriented radially around the pillar and facing towards the rising sun. Several small cross-carved slabs at the site may have served as grave markers.

Many ancient standing stones in Ireland have legends related to them; the story connected to Kilnasaggart suggests there was once a famous cow in the glen that gave milk in abundance. One day a person attempted, when milking the cow, to procure the milk through a sieve. The cow was so angry that she stamped her foot and fled the glen, never to return. The shape of her hoof remains beside this stone to this day.

Landmark fact: The Kilnasaggart Pillar Stone is located on a symbolic ancient road. This ran from Tara in County Meath and through the Moyry Pass to Dunseverick Head on the North Antrim Coast.

Beaghmore Stone Circles, County Tyrone

Beaghmore – *Beach Mór* – meaning Large Birch Wood, is an impressive series of Bronze Age ceremonial stone monuments that was excavated from the surrounding bog between 1945 and 1949 and later during the mid-1960s. Archaeologists believe that this complex of stone circles, alignments and caves, located on the fringe of the Sperrin Mountains, dates back to the early Bronze Age.

It was first excavated by the archaeologist A. McL. May, and this project in the 1940s revealed three pairs of stone circles, all under a metre (3.3 feet) in height, and one circle standing alone which is filled with over 800 stones.

Ten alignments of stones, along with several cairns, were revealed under the peat of this preserved site. The stone circles occur in pairs, with associated small cairns and stone alignments, except for the Dragon's Teeth which is a single large circle filled with 884 closely set stones.

Tulach Óg, County Tyrone

The reopening of the iconic Tulach Óg Fort (*Tullaghoge*, meaning Hill of the Young Warrior) in June 2016 has brought one of Ulster's most notable landmarks back into the public domain. Located on the main Stewartstown to Cookstown road in the east of County Tyrone, this magnificent rounded hilltop enclosure is a site of huge historical and cultural significance.

The site is at an altitude of 91.5 metres (300 feet). It consists of two circular banks, both now covered with trees, commanding wide views and is visible from many kilometres/miles around. Indeed many sixteenth and seventeenth-century English maps of Ulster mark the area. In historic terms, the fort has played an important role in the history not just of Tyrone, but also of Ulster and Ireland.

Originally Tullaghoge was a minor kingdom called Telach Óc, occupied in St Patrick's time by the Uí Thuírtrí, who later moved to the eastern side of the River Bann. The Kings of Airgialla were once inaugurated here, but between 900 and AD 1000 the Cenél nEógain branch of the dynasty of Aileach spread south and east from Inis Eoghain in Donegal through the present-day counties of Derry, Tyrone, Armagh and Fermanagh and established Tulach Óg as the centre of their power.

Indeed, by the eleventh century, Tulach Óg was a dynastic centre and inaugural place for Cenél nEógain (descendants of Eoghan – son of Niall of the Nine Hostages) and from then Tyrone became the traditional stronghold of the various O'Neill clans and families. The first to take O'Neill as their surname was Domhnall, who took the name of his grandfather who was killed in a battle with the Vikings. O'Neill thus translates as 'grandson of Niall'.

Up until the time of Brian Boru, the Uí Néill (descendants of Niall of the Nine Hostages) were, almost without interruption, High Kings of Ireland. They formed two main branches: the northern Uí Néill of Ulster and the southern Uí Néill who established themselves in Meath.

The O'Hagan clan were also prominent at Tullaghoge. They were custodians of the fort and chief justices in the O'Neill political system. The inauguration ceremony at the fort was conducted by throwing a shoe over the head of the new chief, to indicate that he would follow in the footsteps of his distinguished ancestors who had borne the title of the 'O'Neill'.

The ceremony took place on a large boulder known as the *Leac na Rí* which means 'the flagstone of the kings', and legend suggests it was blessed by St Patrick. By the sixteenth century, it had become incorporated into a ceremonial stone chair where three large slabs had been placed around it. It is believed that at the nearby Desertcreat

Church, another part of the stone is incorporated into the porch of that church.

Unfortunately the *Leac na Rí* was destroyed in 1602 during the Nine Years' War by Charles Blount, later known as Lord Mountjoy, in accordance with the Elizabethan policy of destroying all Irish symbols of clan allegiance. This marked the end of the O'Neill reign, with Hugh O'Neill's inauguration in 1595 being the last to take place at Tullaghoge Fort. Often referred to as the Great O'Neill, he fled with members of O'Donnell clan from Donegal to Rome during the Flight of the Earls episode that was considered a major watershed in Irish history.

The official opening of new facilities in 2016 ensured that another milestone in the history of this ancient site had been recorded. In the course of those development works, new and exciting archaeological discoveries were made, including artefacts dating back more than 7,000 years and the foundations of a medieval settlement at the bottom of the hill on which Tullaghoge Fort stands.

Archaeologists working on the site revealed that flint tool fragments were found dating back before 5000 BC to the Mesolithic period, when hunter-gatherer settlers inhabited Ireland.

Landmark fact: Coyle's Cottage is situated about a quarter of a mile from Ardboe Cross; local historians estimate it to be at least 200 years old. It is believed to be the last authentic fisherman's cottage in the area and was inhabited until quite recently. In 1991 the Muinterevlin Historical Society was formed and the cottage's potential was spotted as the perfect place for holding lectures, storytelling and music sessions.

Ardboe Cross, County Tyrone

Ardboe Cross – *Ard Bó, t*he High Place of the Cow – is located in the townland of Farsnagh, close to the mid-point of the western shore of Lough Neagh, marking the area of a monastery associated with St Colman, thought to be founded in the sixth century.

The monastery was destroyed by fire in 1166, but later emerged as the medieval parish church site. This sandstone cross is believed to be the first high cross of Ulster, standing at 5.6 metres (18.5 feet) high and 1 metre (3.5 feet) wide, with twenty-two panels displaying a scheme of biblical carving.

The east (Old Testament) face includes Adam and Eve, the Sacrifice of Isaac and Christ in Glory, with scales and flames beneath. The west (New Testament) side has the Visit of the Magi and the Wedding Feast at Cana, while on the south side of the cross are Cain and Abel, and

David killing Goliath. The scenes on the north side appear to represent scenes from the early life of Christ, including his baptism.

A tenth-century date has been suggested for the erection of Ardboe Cross. There are also the ruins of St Colman's Abbey and a church (believed to have been built in the sixtenth century) in the graveyard.

> **Landmark fact:** The site at Ardboe Cross was the focus for worship during Penal days.

St Patrick's Cross, Carndonagh, County Donegal

Located at the Donagh monastic site near Carndonagh on the Inishowen Peninsula in County Donegal, this eight-feet high cross is also known as the Donagh or St Patrick's Cross. It is thought to have been constructed around AD 650, and is considered one of the most important early-Christian remains in all of Ireland.

The Carndonagh Cross is, however, different from many of the crosses from that era in that it has the crucifixion scene on the shaft of the cross rather than on the head. At the top of the cross there is a beautiful interlacing pattern, which is often used in Celtic art to represent St Patrick's Prayer.

Kilclooney Portal Tomb

The beautiful Kilclooney Dolmen near Ardara in County Donegal dates from around 3500 BC and is regarded as one of the finest examples of a portal tomb anywhere in Ireland. Its impressive capstone measures 4 metres (13 feet) wide, 6 metres (20 feet) long and stands over 1.8 metres (6 feet) high. It is angled like a giant bird preparing to fly. The lower end of the capstone is unusually supported by a small stone, which was placed on top of the backstone. It is believed that this extra stone was placed to allow extra light to shine into the tomb.

Ballylumford Dolmen, County Antrim

This dolmen or portal grave consists of six large stones, standing upright and forming two rows. It is also known as the Druid's Altar and is estimated to be approximately 4,000 years old, and could even be the remains of the chamber of an even older passage tomb. It is based at Islandmagee, a peninsula on Antrim's east coast that lies between Larne Lough and the North Sea between the towns of Larne and Carrickfergus.

CONNACHT

Drumcliff High Cross, County Sligo

Drumcliff or Drumcliffe occupies a stunning location at the foot of the impressive Benbulben Mountain. The remains of the round tower and the elaborately carved high cross highlight the early-Christian heritage of the area, as St Colmcille founded a monastery here in the sixth century.

Adjacent to the ancient graveyard is a road leading to the early nineteenth-century St Columba's Church of Ireland Church and the final resting place of the poet William Butler Yeats (1865–1939). He was originally buried in the south of France, but in accordance with his final wishes, his remains were brought back to Drumcliff in 1948.

W.B. Yeats's headstone bears the last three lines of his poem, Under Ben Bulben:

> Cast a cold eye
> On life, on death,
> Horseman, pass by!

A highly decorated sandstone cross stands on an undecorated plinth. The illustration depicts an excellent example of a figure-sculptured high cross dating to around the tenth century. It is almost 4 metres (13 feet) high.

The east face of the cross shows scenes from the Old Testament, such as a depiction of Adam and Eve with a snake coiled around an apple tree, while the west face shows scenes from the New Testament, including the Crucifixion.

Landmark fact: Beside the road is the stump of a round tower that was struck by lightning in 1396. Tradition says it will ultimately fall on the wisest man who passes it!

Carrowmore Megalithic Cemetery, County Sligo

There are approximately 1,500 recorded megalithic monuments in Ireland, classified into four types: passage tombs, court tombs, portal tombs and wedge tombs.

The largest cemetery of megalithic tombs in Ireland is located at Carrowmore, west of Sligo Town, and is also among the country's oldest – with dates ranging between 4500–3500 BC. Archaeologists have recorded over sixty tombs at this location which covers an area of more than 2.4 kilometres (1.5 miles), of which some thirty are visible today. It is thought originally there may have been more than 100. The largest is Medbh's Cairn – said to be the tomb of Queen Medbh of Connacht.

Most of the monuments are clustered about the large central cairn of Listoghil, with a number of sites trailing off to a dolmen to the north of Carrowmore. This tomb is 34 metres (111 feet) in diameter, and has been completely reconstructed. It stands at the highest point in the cemetery.

Much of the destruction that has taken place at Carrowmore in the past has been due to clearance and road building. As a result, only twenty-five monuments remain today. These are boulder circles, some with a central structure, some with a simple chamber and, in some cases, the remains of a passage.

Excavations by Swedish archaeologists which began in 1977 produced radiocarbon dates that place some of the tombs around 4600 BC, and suggested that the small, simple tombs were probably very early burial places of immigrant farming families.

Landmark fact: Some finds from Carrowmore are on display at the National Museum, Dublin. These include bone pins, a rock crystal pendant and decorated bone fragments.

Rathcroghan, County Roscommon

Rathcroghan, the anglicised version of *Ráth Cruachan*, is a complex of over fifty archaeological monuments near Tulsk village in Roscommon that was of great significance in ancient times as a place of burial and ritual gatherings. Most got their names from the antiquarian, John O'Donovan, who visited Rathcroghan in 1837 while working for the Ordnance Survey.

The royal complex of Cruachan has been nominated to the tentative list for UNESCO World Heritage status. The site is also home to the legendary Cave of the Cats which was described as the entranceway to the 'other world' by fearful Christian scribes.

LEINSTER

Browneshill Dolmen, County Carlow

This dolmen dating from 2500 BC is located to the east of Carlow town and has a granite capstone weighing over 100 tonnes (110.23 tons), making it the largest Neolithic stone formation in Europe.

The massive capstone rests on two portal stones, flanking a door stone and slopes downwards to the west where it rests on a low boulder. It is thought that religious rites were performed at the site for thousands of years, and that it was the burial place of a local king.

Rock of Dunamase, County Laois

The Rock of Dunamase is a naturally occurring limestone rock located in County Laois. It stands at over 45 metres (148 feet) in height and the outcrop with its castle ruins totally dominates the surrounding countryside. The rock overlooks the north-west ridges of the Slieve Bloom Mountains, from where the River Barrow rises. This made the rock a strategic place to build a fortress.

Through the centuries, warriors have fought to control this limestone outcrop, known as a 'hum'. The first known settlement on the rock was *Dún Masc*, an early-Christian settlement that was pillaged by the Vikings. The earliest historical reference to Dunamase is in the *Annals of the Four Masters* where it states that *Dún Masc* was plundered in AD 843 and the Abbot of Terryglass was killed.

Prior to this there are suggestions that Dunamase was known to Ptolemy under the name of Dunum. Although the rock is said to be drawn on a map by the Greek cartographer under that name in the second century, there is no archaeological evidence to support the theory that Dunum is Dunamase.

Later in the twelfth century, when the Normans arrived in Ireland, Dunamase became one of the most important Anglo-Norman strongholds in Laois. It was part of the dowry of Aoife, the daughter of Diarmuid Mac Murrough, King of Leinster, when she was given in marriage to the Norman conqueror Strongbow in 1170.

When Isabel, the daughter of Strongbow and Aoife, wed William Marshal, Earl of Pembroke, Dunamase was given as part of her marriage's wedding gift. It is likely that Marshal carried out some building on the rock when he lived there between 1208 and 1213, though most of the castle is earlier.

The castle was besieged and destroyed by Cromwellian generals in 1651. While there are no contemporary records of these events, it is probably the best explanation for the ruinous state of the castle today.

Landmark fact: Artefacts discovered during recent excavations include several small coins; on the face of one is 'the Morragh' or O'More, and on the reverse side was 'Dunadh', referring to the Rock of Dunamase.

Rathgall, Wicklow

Rathgall is derived from *Ráth Geal*, meaning Bright Fort, and is a hillfort four miles east of Tullow, on the edge of a ridge with four concentric stone walls and extensive panoramic views. It was a royal palace and burial site of the Kings of Leinster.

Rathgall is an imposing monument covering a total area of 7 hectares (18 acres), with the inner circle measuring 15 metres (49 feet) wide. Excavations started in 1969 revealed important evidence for late Bronze Age activity at Rathgall, dating to 800 BC.

Evidence of a house was discovered in the inner stone circle with the second and third ramparts forming the main defensive walls. Other finds included glass, bronze and stone objects, clay moulds, gold and glass beads and other artefacts. It is clear from the excavations that Rathgall was an important site in the later Bronze Age.

Punchestown Longstone, County Kildare

Punchestown Longstone is a standing stone and national monument located near the Punchestown Racecourse in County Kildare. It is the tallest and arguably most striking standing stone in Ireland and was originally tilted. When it toppled in 1931, it was re-erected and found to be nearly 7 metres (23 feet) long and weighed 9 tonnes (9.92 tons). It now stands straight, with a roughly square base, which tapers to a wedge as it nears its apex.

A Bronze Age burial cist was uncovered at the base of this granite stone. Scholars believe that the Punchestown Longstone was constructed by the Beaker people. These were a late Neolithic and early Bronze Age people who migrated through Western Europe, Britain and Ireland from around 2700–1700 BC.

Various functions for the Punchestown Standing Stone have been suggested as possible burial markers, or a boundary stone. There are many tales about the origins of the standing stone at Punchestown and according to local legend, the stone was hurled by the mythical Irish giant and warrior Fionn Mac Cumhaill in a show of strength from the Hill of Allen 11.3 kilometres (7 miles) away.

Monasterboice, County Louth

Muiredach's High Cross is located at the monastic site of Monasterboice (see Chapter 8) and is regarded as the finest high cross in the whole of Ireland. It is named after an abbot, Muiredach mac Domhnaill, who died in 923, and features biblical carvings of both the Old and New Testaments of the Bible. There is an inscription in Irish at the base of the stem: *Or do Muiredach i Chrois*, 'A prayer for Muiredach by whom this cross was made'.

Newgrange, County Meath

Newgrange forms an important part of Brú na Bóinne – Boyne Valley, a UNESCO World Heritage Site in County Meath. The archaeological landscape within Brú na Bóinne is dominated by the three well-known large passage tombs at Knowth, Newgrange and Dowth, built some 5,000 years ago in the Neolithic or late Stone Age.

At Newgrange, the large mound is approximately 80 metres (262 feet) in diameter and 13.5 metres (44 feet) high, while the passage is 19 metres (62 feet) long. Some archaeologists believe the Newgrange site was as high as 58 metres (150 feet) in some areas.

The mound covers a single tomb, which consists of a long passage and a cross-shaped chamber. A corbelled roof covers the chamber. To construct the roof, the builders overlapped layers of large rocks until the roof could be sealed with a capstone, 6 metres (19.5 feet) above the floor.

Remarkably after 5,000 years, the roof at Newgrange is still waterproof. The passage, the chamber and the roof were all constructed, and have survived, without mortar. The passage tomb is surrounded at its base by a kerb of ninety-seven stones.

Arguably the most impressive stone associated with Newgrange is the highly decorated Entrance Stone. Regarded by many as one of the finest achievements of European Neolithic art, another outstanding attraction in the chamber is the world famous tri-spiral design.

The 'roof box' situated above the passage entrance is yet another notable feature associated with this famous landmark. At dawn on the winter solstice, the shortest day of the year, and for a number of days before and after, a shaft of sunlight enters the chamber through an opening in the roof box and penetrates the passage, shining onto the floor of the inner chamber. The beam illuminates the inner chamber of Newgrange for just seventeen minutes. To the Neolithic culture of the Boyne Valley, the winter solstice marked the start of the New Year – a sign of nature's rebirth and promising renewed life to animals and humans.

A circle of standing stones also surrounds Newgrange. Its purpose is unclear, although recent research indicates that it could have had an astronomical function. The stone circle was erected sometime after 2000 BC, since excavations have shown that one of the stones of the circle lies directly on top of the early Bronze Age pit circle, which this was the final phase of building at Newgrange.

After the foundation of the Cistercian Abbey at nearby Mellifont in AD 1142 , the land around the monument was acquired by the order. It became a grange, an outlying farm of the abbey, thus giving the passage tomb and the surrounding townland its modern name.

Newgrange was 'rediscovered' in 1699 by the removal of material for road building. The landowner, Charles Campbell, needed some stones and asked his workers to carry some stones away from the cairn. When those stones were moved, the entrance to the tomb was uncovered.

An extensive archaeological excavation took place at Newgrange from 1962 until 1975, and the roof box was rediscovered in 1963. The protection and conservation of Newgrange and other Brú na Bóinne sites is provided by a range of national legislation and international guidelines; and most of the 780-hectare (1,927-acre) site is in private ownership.

Newgrange attracts almost 200,000 people each year, making it the most visited archaeological monument in Ireland. The Brú na Bóinne Visitor Centre opened to the public in June 1997. It contains exhibitions that describe how the monuments were built; how they were used; where the building stones were found and how these were moved to the site.

> **Landmark fact:** An interesting phenomenon associated with Newgrange is the discovery of Roman coins over the past four centuries. Many have been found at the site, with the first recorded find of a coin in 1699. These Roman coins were still being found in the 1960s when Newgrange was being excavated – some of them in mint condition. Whether they were buried here by native Irish worshippers or pilgrims from the Roman world remains a mystery.

Loughcrew, County Meath

This landmark is somewhat less heralded than its Newgrange neighbour. Situated to the north of the Boyne Valley, near the village of Oldcastle, the tombs at Loughcrew are located on two neighbouring hills – Cairnbane East and Cairnbane West. The whole cemetery is known as *Sliabh na Callighe* – the Hill of the Witch.

Folklore suggests that the monuments at Loughcrew were formed when a witch called *An Cailleach Bhéara* was challenged to drop an apron full of stones on each of the three Loughcrew peaks: if she succeeded she would be proclaimed the ruler of all Ireland. She was successful on the first two peaks, but missed the third and fell to her death.

> **Landmark fact:** The largest of the tombs, Cairn T, stands on the summit of Carnbane East. This passage tomb has some of the finest examples of Neolithic art in Ireland.

MUNSTER

Drombeg Stone Circles, County Cork

Drombeg stone circle – *Droim Beag* in Irish, meaning 'the small ridge' – is located east of Glandore in south-west Cork. Drombeg is one of the best-known archaeological sites in County Cork and is protected under the National Monuments Act. It commands a glorious location at the head of a long green valley, gently gazing towards the Atlantic. This setting is just one of the reasons why it is the most visited stone circle in Ireland.

Before it was excavated by Professor Edward Fahy in 1957, it was known as the Druid's Altar by local people. The circle is a megalithic formation that once consisted of seventeen stones (only thirteen remain); Radiocarbon dating of human remains found at the site during the excavation in the 1950s suggests that the area was built and actively used between 1100–800 BC.

The Drombeg stones are mostly less than 2 metres (6.5 feet) high, and the stone circle is oriented along the south-west axis, to line up with the mid-winter solstice. The most westerly stone, 1.9 metres (6 feet) long, has two egg-shaped cup marks, one with a ring around it.

Dysert O'Dea, County Clare

Located 7 miles north of the county town of Ennis is this monastic foundation of the eighth-century monk St Tola. It was also the scene of an important battle in 1318, when the O'Briens defeated the de Clares of Bunratty, and prevented the Anglo-Norman takeover of County Clare.

Here there are the remains of a twelfth-century Romanesque church and in a field to the east of the church is the 'White Cross of Tola' that contains high relief carvings of Christ and a bishop and Daniel in the Lion's Den, as well as intricate patterning. It was re-erected by Conor O'Dea in 1683, and again by the Synges in 1871.

> **Landmark fact:** Near the north-western corner of the church stand the remains of a round tower. The nearby Dysert O'Dea Castle is a fully restored castellated Gaelic tower-house, built in grey stone over four floors in 1480 by the O'Dea clan.

Ahenny High Crosses, County Tipperary

Located in the ancient monastic site of Kilclispen in a valley running north into the Slievenamon Hills, these are two high crosses that are decorated with a number of well-carved geometrical motifs, such as interlacing and spirals, which are similar in style to the *Book of Kells*.

The crosses are dated to the eighth century, and are part of a group of crosses in a similar style called the Slievenamon Group. Others include Kilkeeran, Kilree and Kilamery in County Kilkenny and Lorrha in County Tipperary. The bases of these crosses are often carved with narrative scenes depicting groups of animals and humans, nature or hunting, processions and battles.

Pillar stones in Munster

Pillar stones are largely found in Munster, in particular in the counties of Cork, Kerry and Waterford. They date from the early centuries of Christianity and some of them provide us with the earliest known written form of the Irish language – Ogham, which uses a series of lines and etches scratched into the corner of pillar stones to create an alphabet. Here are two examples of pillar stones:

Kilnaruane Carved Pillar Stone, County Cork

Sometimes referred to as 'The Bantry Pillar', this early-Christian pillar stone located near Bantry is thought to have formed the shaft of a ninth-century high cross. It stands about 2 metres (7 feet) in height, is 25.5 centimetres (10 inches) wide and 15 centimetres (6 inches) across. It is based on a low earthen platform on a hillcrest and is decorated on one face with weathered scriptural scenes, and on the other with a carving of a primitive boat and crew.

Reask Pillar Stone, County Kerry

This intricately decorated cross-inscribed pillar located on the Dingle Peninsula stands in an old walled monastic enclosure, which also contains two smaller cross-slabs and the foundations of a number of beehive huts.

This particular pillar measures 1.64 metres (5.3 feet) in height and is 0.6 metres (1.96 feet) wide and is decorated with an encircled Greek cross from which pendant spiral designs emanate. The stone was decorated in early-Christian times, around the seventh century.

7

THE URBAN LANDSCAPE

Despite the hustle and bustle of large towns and cities in Ireland, one cannot fail to notice the magnificence of the many landmarks that exist. In Irish cities there is a plethora of famous landmark buildings and open spaces – such as the Mansion House in Dublin and Eyre Square in Galway. In other cities such as Belfast, the City Hall is a versatile landmark that even hosts a popular market twice a year!

There are also world-famous sporting arenas such as Croke Park (Dublin) and Thomond Park (Limerick) that have a fascinating history; while new buildings, bridges and monuments such as the Peace Bridge in Derry are symbolic of a confident twenty-first-century Ireland.

ULSTER

Armagh
Ard Mhacha meaning Macha's Height, was named after Queen Macha who built a fortress on the main hill where the Church of Ireland cathedral now stands. It is one of the oldest settlements in Ireland and was located on the Moyry Pass, which once stretched from the south of Ireland, through Tara, to the north.

Armagh is the only city in the world with two cathedrals dedicated to the one saint, in this case St Patrick. It is known as the ecclesiastical capital of Ireland because of its status as the seat of the Archbishops of Armagh and the Primates of All Ireland for both the Roman Catholic Church and the Church of Ireland.

The Mall, Armagh

The Mall has been central to the leisure activities of Armagh's citizens for over 200 years. This tree-lined promenade was created in the early eighteenth century, and from 1731 until 1773 it was a horse-racing course, with monthly trading fairs in the central area.

In 1765, the Church of Ireland Archbishop Robinson began a plan to redevelop Armagh as a city to rival Dublin. He gifted the new mall to the citizens of Armagh as a public walkway. Over the years this Orchard County landmark became an area for sports such as cricket, football and rugby.

The Mall remains a popular venue for residents of Armagh and surrounding villages to use its marvellous facilities for leisure and recreation purposes. The ground is used for club games by Armagh Cricket Club; in 2005 the ground hosted an international cricket competition for the ICC Trophy between Denmark and the United States

Another feature of the Mall is 'The Turning Point', a bronze public sculpture which was removed from the former St Anne's Square in Belfast. It was redeveloped and installed in March 2012. The artwork takes the form of a 2.5-metre (8-foot) diameter bronze globe surrounded and supported by four figures (two male and two female), in the form of negative life-casts.

Landmark fact: In 2005 the Mall won an Irish Architecture Award for its restoration of the urban park.

Belfast

Béal Feirste, meaning 'river mouth of the sandy ford', is the second largest city in Ireland. It became a substantial settlement by the seventeenth century after being established as a town by Sir Arthur Chichester. It flourished as a commercial and industrial centre over the next two centuries, with linen and shipbuilding prominent in its success.

Stormont

Following the Government of Ireland Act of 1920, Belfast needed to acquire a parliament house and headquarters buildings for government departments. From September 1921 until June 1932, the Parliament of Northern Ireland met in Assembly's College in Botanic Avenue, Belfast (later known as Union Theological College). On 20 September 1921, the Parliament of Northern Ireland had voted its approval of the Stormont Castle demesne as the location for the new parliament houses and ministerial buildings, and the site was purchased for the sum of £20,334.

The design and construction of Stormont was a huge task and eventually amounted to a total cost of £1.2 million. On 16 November 1932, the opening ceremony was performed by the Prince of Wales, and the following week the first parliamentary session in the new building commenced.

The layout of Parliament Buildings is dominated by the great ceremonial spaces of the Central Hall, the Assembly (Commons) Chamber and the Senate Chamber, all in the core of the building. The main entrance is on the south front, but there are also imposing entrances on the east and west fronts, all marble-lined and beautifully detailed.

The superb landscaped setting was specifically conceived on a grand scale to enhance the grandeur of the building. The straight processional drive ascends for some 54 metres (180 feet) over a distance of almost 1.6 kilometres (1 mile) from the entrance gates to the south. The imposing statue of Ulster Unionist leader Edward Carson stands 9.75 metres (32 feet) high on level ground on the way up to the 27.5-metre (90-foot) wide granite steps, which rise to the central doors of the building.

Since its completion, Parliament Buildings has functioned as the seat of a legislature, or other elected body when such have been in existence, and as headquarter offices for various government departments.

In the early hours of 2 January 1995, a major fire caused extensive damage, and the Commons Chamber was totally burnt out, but the adjoining rooms and corridors, though heavily smoke-stained, survived surprisingly unscathed. A few months later, it was announced that the chamber would be completely restored in conjunction with the overall upgrading, re-servicing and reorganising of the building.

Under the terms of the Good Friday Agreement of 10 April 1998, a Northern Ireland Assembly was elected and sat for the first time in Parliament Buildings on 14 September that year. The current area of the estate is 164 hectares (407 acres) and is open to the public 365 days a year.

Landmark fact: During the Second World War, the entire Stormont building was covered in dark camouflage paint, and part of it was taken over by the Royal Air Force (RAF).

Belfast City Hall

Belfast was granted city status by Queen Victoria in 1888. This prompted the Belfast Corporation (later known as Belfast City Council) to commission a city hall to celebrate this new status. A young Englishmen named Alfred Brumwell Thomas was selected because his design was so unlike typical Victorian buildings at the time.

Funding for the City Hall was raised with the profits of Belfast Gasworks, for which the Belfast Corporation was responsible. Construction began in 1898 and was completed in 1906, opening its doors on 1 August 1906. The building was scheduled to cost £150,000, but the final bill was £360,000.

Tours of Belfast City Hall were free, as the council decided that the citizens of Belfast had already paid for it once and it would not be fair to charge them again, and this feature has continued to the present day. The inside of the City Hall houses dozens of paintings, busts, statues and stained-glass windows to commemorate important aspects of Belfast's history. In 1959, the original Titanic Memorial Monument, designed by Sir Thomas Brock, was moved to the grounds of City Hall.

Now known as the Titanic Memorial Garden, this area of the grounds stands in memory of the 'dutiful and heroic members of Belfast who died saving the lives of hundreds of people' on board the ship. A plinth in memory of citizens who died also stands in the garden. Another connection between City Hall and *Titanic* is the Lord Mayor's Suite – also known as the Titanic Rooms as craftsmen who worked on them went on to work on the famous liner.

In recent years, Belfast City Hall has undergone major developments, such as an £11 million refurbishment programme. On 12 October 2009, the then United States Secretary of State Hilary Clinton performed a ribbon-cutting ceremony and unveiled a plaque to mark the reopening of the landmark.

Landmark fact: Belfast City Hall suffered a direct hit during the Belfast Blitz of the Second World War. While examining the wreckage, one lone painting was discovered: a portrait of a previous mayor of the City Hall.

Titanic Building

Housed in an iconic, six-storey building, Titanic Belfast is located in the heart of the city, beside the historic site of this world-famous ship's construction, only 100 metres (109 yards) from where *Titanic* was constructed and launched. To its right is the Harland & Wolff

Drawing Office where she was designed and to the left is the Victoria Channel from where she first set sail.

Construction of this project commenced in May 2009, and the architecturally unique building opened to critical acclaim on 31 March 2012, in time for the centenary of the *Titanic*'s ill-fated voyage. The massive 14,000 square metre (16,750 square yards) structure (twice the size of Belfast City Hall) accommodates nine galleries of interactive exhibition space. The impressive façade is clad in 3,000 different shaped silver aluminium panels that create an impressive visual appearance, enhanced by reflective pools of water surrounding the base.

The proximity of the historic Titanic Slipways and the Harland & Wolff Drawing Offices were central considerations during the design, planning and construction of the project. These heritage elements are valuable historical monuments and listed buildings. The total cost of the *Titanic* building project was in excess of £100 million. It is the most expensive tourism project ever completed in Northern Ireland.

Landmark fact: Titanic Belfast was the winner of the prestigious Europe's Leading Visitor Attraction (World Travel Awards, 2016).

Harland & Wolff Cranes – Samson and Goliath

The two massive cranes in Harland & Wolff Belfast that serve one of the world's largest building docks are certainly masterpieces of engineering. The cranes, which were named after the Biblical figures Samson and Goliath, dominate the Belfast skyline and are landmark structures of the city. The first, Goliath, was completed in July 1969 and was largely constructed by Harland & Wolff within the company, while the second, Samson, was provided by the German engineering firm Krupp in its entirety and was completed in May 1974.

In most respects the cranes are identical, but Samson is some 10 metres (32 feet) higher at 106 metres (347 feet) than Goliath's 96 metres (315 feet). Each has a span of 140 metres (460 feet) and a safe working load of 840 tonnes (925 tons).

The Harland & Wolff shipyard was founded in 1862 by Edward James Harland and Gustav Wilhelm Wolff, both shipbuilders and politicians. At its height, Harland & Wolff became one of the biggest shipbuilders in the world. Harland & Wolff constructed over seventy ships for the White Star Line; the *Titanic* was the best known of these.

Between 1900 and 1930, Harland & Wolff was Belfast's biggest employer. Nowadays the yard has restructured itself to focus less on shipbuilding and more on design and structural engineering.

Landmark fact: Samson and Goliath are now much-beloved Belfast landmarks and their future was assured in 1995 when they were scheduled as historic monuments and archaeological objects thanks to a Northern Ireland Government order.

Linen Hall Library

The Linen Hall Library is a truly unique institution. Founded in 1788, it is the oldest library in Belfast and the last subscribing library in Ireland. It was founded as the Belfast Reading Society, and soon became known as the Belfast Society for Promoting Knowledge. In encouraging such interest, the society published Edmund Bunting's *Ancient Irish Music* (1796), the first publication in score form of traditional Irish music.

In 1802, the library secured its first permanent premises in rooms below the clock tower of the White Linen Hall on the site of the present-day City Hall – hence the origins of the library's present-day name.

In 1888, at the time of its centenary, the library faced a crisis, with the prospective loss of its home in the White Linen Hall to make way for the new City Hall. The purchase of the library's present main building at Donegall Square North ensured a permanent and secure base for the future. It is renowned for its unparalleled Irish and local studies collection, ranging from comprehensive holdings of early Belfast and Ulster printed books to the 250,000 items in the Northern Ireland Political Collection.

Nowadays, the Linen Hall has an illustrious profile as a centre of cultural and creative life and offers a varied programme of events, ranging from monthly exhibitions to readings and lectures.

Landmark fact: The second librarian, Thomas Russell, was a leading member of the Society of United Irishmen and was arrested on the library premises in 1796 for inciting rebellion and later executed in Downpatrick on 21 October 1803.

Derry

Doire, meaning 'Oak Grove', like other cities in Ireland, has a rich and interesting history. Ptolemy's map of Ireland in AD 140 made reference to Derry's River Foyle (it was referred to as the Widwa). In AD 546 St Columba is said to have originally founded Derry city and to have built a monastery on the bank of the River Foyle.

In 1613, the city was granted a royal charter by King James I and gained the 'London' prefix (Londonderry) to reflect the funding of the construction of the new city on the Foyle's west bank by the London livery companies.

City Walls

Derry is the only remaining completely walled city in Ireland and one of the finest examples of walled cities in Europe. The walls were built during the period 1613–1618 as defences for early seventeenth-century settlers from England and Scotland.

The walls, which are two-storey ramparts of earth and stone 1.6 kilometres (1 mile) long, form a walkway around the inner city and provide a unique promenade to view the layout of the original town, which still preserves its Renaissance-style street plan. The four original gates to the walled city are Bishop's Gate, Ferryquay Gate, Butcher Gate and Shipquay Gate. Three further gates were added: Magazine Gate, Castle Gate and New Gate.

Beyond the latter gate, the Church of Ireland cathedral comes into view with its tower projecting above the walls. During the Siege of Derry in 1689, the tower was given wooden platforms for the defenders to use.

> **Landmark fact:** The city claims Europe's largest collection of cannon. In 2005, the surviving twenty-four cannon were restored, and under expert supervision and often by hand, craftsmen brought the cannon back to their former glory. The cannon are displayed throughout the city walls with the impressive 'Roaring Meg' located on the double bastion.

Peace Bridge

At a cost of £14.6 million, the Millennium Bridge across the River Foyle in Londonderry/Derry opened on 25 June 2011. The total length of the bridge is 312 metres (1,023 feet) and is designed for pedestrians and cyclists. It stretches from Guildhall Square on the west bank to Ebrington on the east bank.

The Peace Bridge is the newest of three bridges in the city, the others being the Craigavon Bridge and the Foyle Bridge, and it took only eighteen months to build. The Peace Bridge was designed by Wilkinson Eyre Architects who also designed the Gateshead Millennium Bridge over the River Tyne in England.

Around 1,000 tonnes of steel were used in the construction, the equivalent of 143 double decker buses. Due to the complex 'S' shape of the bridge deck, each section had to be constructed and connected to the next section in sequence at the factory in Newport, Wales, to ensure that when they arrived in the city they would all fit together perfectly on site.

The bridge was opened to the public by EU Commissioner for Regional Policy, Johannes Hahn; accompanied by the then First and Deputy First Ministers for Northern Ireland, Peter Robinson and Martin McGuinness, as well as the Irish Taoiseach, Enda Kenny.

> **Landmark fact:** 4.5 kilometres (2.8 miles) of electric cable were laid on the bridge – enough to go around Derry's City Walls three times.

The Guildhall

The Guildhall is located in the heart of Derry city, on the edge of the city walls and close to the Peace Bridge. Fashioned in neo-Gothic style, this famous landmark was originally built in 1890, and then rebuilt after a fire in 1908. The entire interior of the building was badly damaged by two bombs in 1972, but was restored at a cost of £1.7 million and reopened five years later.

The Guildhall is noted for its fine stained-glass windows, presented by the London livery companies, and its clocktower, which is modelled on London's Big Ben at Westminster. A major £9.5 million restoration of the Guildhall was completed in June 2013, and while retaining its civic function it now also boasts a new multifaceted tourism experience, providing a central hub for visitors exploring the city.

> **Landmark fact:** In July 2016 the Derry Guildhall welcomed its 1 millionth visitor since its restoration in 2013.

LEINSTER

Dublin

Baile Átha Cliath (Town of the Hurdles) is the capital city of Ireland. Founded as a Viking settlement, it became Ireland's main population base following the Anglo-Norman invasion during the late twelfth century.

On 24 April 1916, the Easter Rising took place in Dublin. The insurgents occupied the General Post Office (GPO) in O'Connell Street where the leader Patrick Pearse announced an Irish Republic. The prosperity of the so-called 'Celtic Tiger' era of the mid-1990s to the mid-2000s created many new buildings and landmarks around the city, including the Spire that was erected on O'Connell Street.

Historic O'Connell Street

O'Connell Street in central Dublin is half-a-kilometre long and contains a number of the most famous historical landmarks in Ireland. Formerly named Sackville Street after Lionel Sackville, Viceroy of Ireland and the first Duke of Dorset, it was renamed in honour of Kerryman Daniel O'Connell, the famous nineteenth-century barrister and nationalist leader, whose monument stands at the lower end of the street, facing O'Connell Bridge. The street also contains statues of notable figures from Irish history, such as James Joyce, Jim Larkin and Charles Stewart Parnell.

The city's main thoroughfare (and officially the widest) is synonymous with the 1916 Easter Rising. The General Post Office was gutted by fire and shelling during that week over a century ago. It was rebuilt in 1929 and continues to function as a post office. The front façade of the building is scarred with bullet holes from the Rising as well as the Irish Civil War.

The Monument of Light (the Spire)

Outside the GPO once stood Nelson's Pillar, erected in 1808. This impressive Doric column, topped by a statue of Lord Admiral Nelson, was destroyed by explosion in 1966 – and 'the Spire' now graces the site of where Nelson's Pillar was situated. Completed on 21 January 2003, this 121-metre (398-feet) high stainless steel spire is officially known as the Monument of Light. At the time of completion it was believed to be the tallest piece of freestanding sculpture in the world.

Tapering from 3 metres (9.8 feet) in diameter at its base to a mere 10 centimetres (4 inches) in the sky, it is lit internally at its tip and by projections of light from surrounding buildings for most of its height. It has received some witty and imaginative alternative titles from Dubliners such as 'the Stiletto in the Ghetto' and is meant to represent an icon of modernity in twenty-first-century Ireland.

Trinity College and the *Book of Kells*

Dublin University or Trinity College Dublin (TCD) was founded in 1592 by a royal charter granted by Queen Elizabeth I. At the time it was hoped that the establishment of a university in Dublin would be instrumental in bringing Ireland into the mainstream of European learning and strengthening the Protestant Reformation within Ireland.

Nowadays the city centre campus occupies some 20.6 hectares (51 acres), and the main entrance to the college is located on College Green, opposite the former Irish Houses of Parliament (now Bank of Ireland), and its grounds are bounded by Nassau Street, Lincoln Place, Westland Row and Pearse Street.

The western side of the college is older, featuring the iconic Campanile – a bell tower and one of the most famous landmarks in central Dublin, sculpted by Thomas Kirk and finished in 1853.

Famous TCD alumni include Nobel Prize winners Ernest Walton and Samuel Beckett, as well as Oscar Wilde and Mary Robinson – the President of Ireland from 1990 to 1997.

The *Book of Kells* was written around AD 800. It is a book of the gospels written by hand by monks and beautifully illuminated. The book is housed in the Long Room in the Old Library of Trinity College, Dublin.

Also housed in the Library is the *Book of Durrow* – a manuscript gospel book dating from between 650 and AD 680 – predating the *Book of Kells* by over a century.

Landmark fact: A Trinity College superstition holds that any student who passes beneath the Campanile when the bells toll will fail their exams, causing some to never pass under it until they finish their time at the university.

Kilmainham Gaol

Built in 1792, Kilmainham Gaol has held some of the most famous Nationalist and Republican leaders – such as the 1916 protagonists Padraig Pearse and Thomas Clarke. Éamon de Valera, who subsequently became Taoiseach (Prime Minister) and President of Ireland, was the very last prisoner to be incarcerated at the site. He was released in July 1924.

Kilmainham Gaol first operated as the new county gaol for Dublin, and it was in this role that it held thousands of ordinary men, women and children in the late eighteenth and nineteenth centuries. Their crimes ranged from petty offences such as stealing food to more serious crimes such as murder. Convicts from many parts of Ireland were held at the prison for long periods, waiting to be transported to Australia.

The executions of the leaders of the 1916 Easter Rising in the prison yard created a huge level of support for Irish Nationalism. The guided tour tells the tales of prisoners such as Joseph Mary Plunkett, who married Grace Gifford by candlelight in the prison chapel just before he faced the firing squad and James Connolly, who was unable to stand up due to his wounds, so he was tied to a chair for his execution.

Kilmainham Gaol closed its doors as a penal facility in 1924. The building is one of the largest unoccupied prisons in Europe and presents the rough conditions as they were. This location topped the Trip Advisor list of Top 10 Irish landmarks for 2016 – for the fourth year in a row. It is now a museum operated and managed by the Office of Public Works (OPW).

Landmark fact: Kilmainham Gaol has been featured as a backdrop in films such as *Michael Collins* (1996) and *In the Name of the Father* (1993).

Ha'penny Bridge, Dublin

Pedestrians wishing to cross the river in the Temple Bar area of Dublin city can use either the Millennium Bridge or the Ha'penny Bridge. The Ha'penny Bridge was built in 1816 and was originally known as the Wellington Bridge, after the Dublin-born Duke of Wellington. The name changed to Liffey Bridge – and this remains the bridge's official name to this day, although it is most commonly referred to as the Ha'penny Bridge.

It has a 43-metre (141-foot) span, is 3 metres (9.8 feet) in width and rises 3 metres (9.8 feet) above the river. The name 'Ha'penny Bridge' comes from the toll that was originally charged to cross the bridge. The cost of the toll was the equivalent of the price paid for the ferry across the river before the bridge was constructed. It retained its position as the only pedestrian bridge to span the river until the opening of the Millennium Bridge in 1999. Nowadays, an average of 30,000 people cross the bridge every day.

Landmark fact: The toll fee to cross the bridge was paid to William Walsh, ferry owner and alderman of the city. He retired his leaking river ferries and was compensated with £3,000 and the bridge lease for 100 years.

Glasnevin Cemetery, Dublin

The suburb of Glasnevin is 3.2 kilometres, or a couple of miles, north of O'Connell Street, and its Prospect Cemetery is a famous landmark that receives thousands of visitors each year. This is due to the historically notable monuments and the graves of many of Ireland's most prominent national figures such as Charles Stewart Parnell, Michael Collins and Éamon de Valera, who are buried in Glasnevin.

Prior to the establishment of Glasnevin Cemetery, Irish Catholics had no cemeteries of their own in which to bury their dead and, as the repressive Penal Laws of the eighteenth century placed heavy restrictions on the public performance of Catholic services, it had become normal practice for Catholics to conduct a limited version of their own funeral services in Protestant churchyards or graveyards.

However, after an incident in 1825 at St Kevin's Cemetery, Camden Row, Dublin, which saw an overzealous sexton caution a Catholic priest who attempted to say a limited form of a requiem Mass, Daniel O'Connell, champion of Catholic rights, launched a campaign that advocated the opening of a burial ground in which both Irish Catholics and Protestants could give their dead dignified burial.

Thus Glasnevin Cemetery was consecrated and opened to the public for the first time on 21 February 1832. The cemetery was initially known as Prospect Cemetery, a name chosen from the townland of Prospect, which surrounded the cemetery lands. Originally covering 3.6 hectares (9 acres) of ground, the area of the cemetery has now grown to approximately 50 hectares (124 acres).

As Ireland's first 'National Cemetery' it contains a number of important landmarks within it. There is a 45.7-metre (150-foot) high round tower that marks the tomb of the cemetery's founder and one of Ireland's major historical figures, Daniel O'Connell.

> **Landmark fact:** The high wall with watchtowers surrounding the main part of Glasnevin Cemetery was built to deter The Resurrection Men (also known as bodysnatchers), who were active in Dublin in the eighteenth and early nineteenth centuries. The watchmen also had a pack of bloodhounds who roamed the cemetery at night.

Croke Park

Croke Park is the headquarters of the Gaelic Athletics Association (GAA), the largest sporting body in Ireland. Prior to the association's purchase of the stadium in 1913, the grounds were in private ownership. The rebuilding of the stadium on Jones's Road (there had been a smaller sportsground on the site in previous years) led to it being named Croke Park in honour of Archbishop Thomas Croke (1824–1902) – the first patron of the GAA.

Croke Park has subsequently grown from a humble sports ground on the edge of Dublin to become the most famous sports stadium in Ireland. It is one of the largest sporting arenas in Europe, with a capacity of 82,300 and can accommodate all types of events – from field sports to concerts.

Indeed, Croke Park has UEFA and FIFA approved certification and has hosted numerous high-profile international sporting, cultural and music events outside of the Gaelic Games. International musicians such as Bon Jovi and Bruce Springsteen have played at the famous north Dublin venue.

A huge debt of gratitude for the stadium's very existence goes to a County Limerick native, Frank Dineen, who erected the ground's first stadium terracing and invested in modernising the grounds that the Gaelic Athletics Association benefitted from when they purchased the venue in 1913 from Dineen for £3,500.

In 1917, rubble from the previous year's Easter Rising was used to construct a grassy hill on the railway end of Croke Park. This terrace became known as Hill 16. A dark day for Croke Park came on Bloody Sunday, 21 November 1920, when fourteen people were killed in Croke Park as they attended a challenge football match between Dublin and Tipperary. The Hogan Stand was named after one of those killed that day – Tipperary captain Michael Hogan.

The Cusack Stand (in honour of GAA founder Michael Cusack) was built in 1938, and the Nally Stand (after Pat Nally, another GAA founder) in 1952. Talks of a redeveloped Croke Park began in the 1980s and the design for an 80,000 capacity stadium was completed in 1991.

The fulfilment of these well-laid plans in 2005 formed the stadium that Irish people are proud of – a hugely important symbol of Irish identity. Another historic first for Croke Park came in January 2006, when it was announced that the GAA had reached agreement with the Football Association of Ireland and the Irish Rugby Football Union to stage Six Nations games and soccer internationals at Croke Park for the first time.

Croke Park has also hosted the opening and closing ceremonies of the Special Olympics World Summer Games in 2003, the first time these events were held outside the United States.

Landmark fact: The largest attendance at Croke Park was in 1961 when 90,556 people watched Down defeat Offaly in the All-Ireland Football Final.

Mansion House, Dawson Street

The Mansion House was constructed by Joshua Dawson in 1710, a property developer after whom Dawson Street (where this landmark is located) is named. He intended it to be his own house, but at the time the Dublin City Assembly was looking for an official residence for the Lord Mayor. So, on 25 April 1715, Dublin Corporation purchased the Mansion House at a cost of £3,500 and also agreed to pay a yearly rent to Joshua Dawson of 40 shillings and a loaf of double-refined sugar weighing 6lb each Christmas.

In return, Dawson agreed to build an extra room to the house, which could be used for civic receptions. Since then, this iconic venue has been the centre of the city's civic life for three centuries.

Dublin was the first city in Ireland or Britain to have an official residence for its lord mayor. The Mansion House itself is still home to the First Citizen of Dublin during his or her term of office, which lasts for one year.

The Round Room was purpose designed in 1821 to receive King George IV. Remarkable political events have taken place here, including the first ever meeting of Dáil Eireann in 1919, and throughout the years this famous Dublin landmark has proudly welcomed high-profile international guests, including Pope John Paul II, Nelson Mandela and Princess Grace of Monaco.

In 1921, 100 years after the room was built to receive the British monarch, the Anglo-Irish Treaty was ratified here. This ended the Anglo-Irish War, declaring Ireland as a Free State.

> **Landmark fact:** Important civic events held in the Mansion House include the conferring of the Honorary Freedom of the city of Dublin, and there have been seventy-eight people granted this (as of April 2017).

Phoenix Park

Phoenix Park is 709 hectares (1,752 acres) and was officially opened to the public in 1745. It is the largest enclosed urban public park in Europe, and is more than twice the size of New York City's Central Park.

The name 'Phoenix' does not derive from the legendary bird, but instead is thought to be a version of the Irish *fionn uisce*, meaning 'clear water'.

There are a number of important buildings in the park, including Áras an Uachtaráin, the official residence of the President of Ireland, located near the centre of the park. When Mary Robinson became the first woman to be elected President in 1990, she started the practice of keeping a light shining in a window of Áras an Uachtaráin as a sign of welcome home and as a remembrance of Irish people all over the world.

The oldest building in the park is Ashtown Castle, a restored medieval tower-house dating from the fifteenth century. There are a number of memorials and monuments in the park, with the largest of these being the Wellington Monument, which stands at 63 metres (206 feet). The Phoenix Column is in the centre of the park and is believed to mark the site of a spring of clear water from where the park gets its name.

Dublin Zoo is located within the environs of Phoenix Park. Opened in 1831 by the Royal Zoological Society of Ireland, which had been founded the previous year, it is the second oldest zoo in Europe. Also located close to the zoo is the US ambassador to Ireland's residence.

Phoenix Park has also played host to music concerts over the years, and among the artists that have performed there were the legendary Dublin group U2.

> **Landmark fact:** The Phoenix Park played host to one of the biggest gatherings of Irish people ever to take place. On Saturday 29 September 1979 it is estimated that 1.25 million people assembled in the park for the visit of Pope John Paul II.

St James's Gate Brewery and the Guinness Storehouse

St James's Gate Brewery was founded in 1759 in Dublin by Arthur Guinness. Originally leased at £45 per year for 9,000 years, St James's Gate has been the home of Guinness ever since.

The original brewery was only 1.6 hectares (4 acres) in size, disused, and had little brewing equipment; however, the area was already home to several similar small breweries due to its good supply of water. Arthur Guinness began by brewing ale and quickly built up a successful trade – within a decade he had begun to export his ale to England. It became the largest brewery in Ireland in 1838, and the largest in the world by 1886, with an annual output of 1.2 million barrels. By the turn of the twentieth century, Guinness had become an international brand.

Nowadays at St James's Gate, there is an attached exhibition on the history of Guinness, called the 'Guinness Storehouse', and it is Dublin's most popular tourist attraction. This incorporates elements from the old brewing factory to explain the history of Guinness production. The exhibition takes place over seven floors, in a building the shape of a 14-million-pint glass of Guinness.

Landmark fact: The final floor in the Guinness Storehouse is the Gravity Bar, which has an almost complete 360-degree view over the city.

Chester Beatty Library

The Chester Beatty Library is one of Ireland's unique cultural institutions. A library and art museum, it is located in the secluded gardens of Dublin Castle (see Chapter 5) and houses an impressive collection of rare and valuable artefacts collected by its founder, Alfred Chester Beatty.

Organised around exhibition galleries and reading rooms, the collections are displayed in two permanent exhibitions – 'Sacred Traditions' and 'Artistic Traditions'. The Artistic Traditions Gallery on the first floor exhibits primarily works of art on paper, techniques of printmaking, binding and papermaking and the art of miniature painting.

'Arts of the Book' is a permanent exhibition of almost 600 objects from the library's collections that displays books from the ancient world, including the world-famous Love Poems (*c.* 1160 BC), Egyptian Books of the Dead and beautifully illuminated European manuscripts.

The Sacred Traditions Gallery on the second floor of the library exhibits the sacred texts, illuminated manuscripts and miniature paintings from the great religions and systems of belief represented in the collections – Christianity, Islam and Buddhism, with smaller displays on Confucianism, Daoism, Sikhism and Jainism.

The Islamic Collection includes more than 260 illuminated copies of the Qur'an and manuscript fragments dating from the ninth to the nineteenth century. This collection marks the library as one of the main centres for the study of Islamic culture and arts in the western hemisphere.

The 'Papyrus Collection' includes some of the oldest and most important biblical manuscripts in the world. The texts contain both Old and New Testament books and date from AD 200 to AD 400. They were written in Greek on papyri in Egypt, and were said to have been found on the banks of the Nile in 1929.

Among them is the Book of Numbers, which was the oldest surviving version of a book of the Bible until the Dead Sea Scrolls were unearthed in the mid-twentieth century. The Book of Numbers is the earliest manuscript within the Chester Beatty Biblical Papyri collection.

There is also the oldest manuscript of Paul's letters (dated AD 200) and the oldest surviving book containing all four Gospels and the Acts of the Apostles. Parts of the collection are already on permanent display in the library, and with this wealth of material it isn't surprising that the library has become one of the major centres in the world for the study of the Christian Bible.

It is apt that the library's mission statement seeks to promote 'the appreciation and understanding of world cultures, and the engagement with the peoples whose cultures are represented in the Collections'. These collections were entrusted to the care of the State by Alfred Chester Beatty (1875–1968), who was a successful American mining engineer, collector and philanthropist.

With his son already established on his own estate in Ireland, Beatty relocated to Dublin in 1950, taking the bulk of his collection and his staff with him. Collected over sixty years, the Beatty collection was regarded in that era as one of the finest private collections in the world and certainly one of the last great book collections to be assembled by one individual.

The original Chester Beatty Library, which houses the collection, was built on Shrewsbury Road in Ballsbridge, opening on 8 August 1953; but because it had limited facilities for conservation and inadequate facilities at its disposal to display elements of Beatty's collection for maximum effect, the library relocated to the more centrally located Dublin Castle in 2000.

As the only museum in Ireland to win 'European Museum of the Year' (in 2002) and rated consistently in the top five of TripAdvisor's list of 'Top things to do in Dublin', the library continues to be an important cultural landmark in the city.

Landmark fact: There were over 340,000 visitors to the Chester Beatty Library during 2015.

Leinster House

Located on Kildare Street in Dublin, Leinster House was built in 1745 as a town house for James Fitzgerald, the Duke of Leinster. It was designed by the architect Richard Cassels, and it has been claimed that it formed a model for the design of the White House in Washington DC.

The house was sold by Augustus Frederick, the 3rd Duke of Leinster to the Royal Dublin Society in 1815 for £10,000 and became their headquarters. At the end of the nineteenth century, two new wings were added, to house the National Library of Ireland and the

National Museum of Ireland. The Natural History Museum was also built on the site.

After the establishment of the Irish Free State in 1922, it was chosen as the seat of Parliament because it was considered easy to defend during the Civil War. The Oireachtas (Irish Parliament), including Dáil Éireann (the House of Representatives), is still housed here as well as the Irish Senate (Seanad Éireann), the National Museum and the National Library.

The Royal Dublin Society had made extensive additions to the house, most notably the lecture theatre, later to become the Dáil Chamber. The entire building was acquired by the State in 1924.

> **Landmark fact:** The first balloon ascent in Ireland was made in July 1783 by Richard Crosbie from the front lawn of Leinster House.

Molly Malone Statue

The popular song 'Cockles and Mussels' has become closely associated with Dublin. The song's fictional protagonist Molly Malone and her barrow represent one of the most familiar symbols of the city. Molly Malone worked as a fishmonger and died in one of the outbreaks of cholera that regularly used to sweep the city of Dublin.

The statue of Molly Malone was designed by Jeanne Rynhart and located on Grafton Street, just a short walk from Trinity College. The unveiling of the statue celebrated Dublin's first millennium in 1988.

Since 18 July 2014, the statue has been relocated to Suffolk Street in order to make way for Luas (Dublin's light rail system) track-laying work to be completed at the old location. It is expected to be returned to its original location in late 2017.

St Stephen's Green

St Stephen's Green park is a historical park and garden, located in the centre of Dublin adjacent to one of the city's main shopping streets, Grafton Street. Cared for by the Office of Public Works, the park provides an idyllic escape from the busy city. The 9-hectare (22-acre) park is filled with lush gardens, beautiful flower beds and a variety of sculptures and monuments.

The name St Stephen's Green originates from a church called St Stephen's in that area in the thirteenth century. In 1663, the Dublin Corporation decided that the plot of ground could be used to generate income for the city and a central area of 11 hectares (27 acres) was marked out which would define the park boundary, with the remaining ground being let out into ninety building lots.

For a time, access to the green was restricted to local residents, but in 1877, the Irish Parliament passed an Act to reopen St Stephen's Green to the public. Lord Ardilaun (Sir A.E. Guinness) played a significant role in the planning and importing of the exotic trees and plants that were installed in the park, and gave it to the Corporation for public use. The current landscape of the park was designed by William Sheppard, and officially opened to the public on 27 July 1880.

St Stephen's Green hosts a large number of important sculptural monuments, which includes: the Fusiliers' Arch at the Grafton Street corner which commemorates the Royal Dublin Fusiliers who died in the Second Boer War; a bronze statue at the Merrion Row corner of Theobald Wolfe Tone, the leader of the 1798 rebellion; and a seated statue of Lord Ardilaun on the western side, facing the Royal College of Surgeons which he also sponsored.

This famous Dublin landmark has been central to many important events in the history of Dublin since its reopening. One such episode occurred on Easter Monday 1916, when one group of the Irish Citizen Army under the command of Michael Mallin and Constance Markiewicz seized control of St Stephen's Green.

Landmark fact: Bullet holes from the fighting during the Rising can still be found today on the Fusiliers' Arch.

Aviva Stadium

The Aviva Stadium is one of Ireland's most famous sporting landmarks, and is located in the Ballsbridge area of south Dublin. This new stadium, home to the Irish rugby team and Republic of Ireland national football team, was officially opened on 14 May 2010, and replaced the former Lansdowne Road Stadium, which had been in existence since the early 1870s – and was thought to be the oldest sports stadium in Europe.

The creation of the original Lansdowne Road Stadium was the brainchild of Henry William Dunlop, an outstanding athlete who organised the first All-Ireland Athletics Championships. His vision was to create a purpose-built sporting venue – and this vision was realised when the stadium first opened for athletics in 1872.

While the original Lansdowne Road Stadium was a multi-sports venue, in 1878 Lansdowne held its first international rugby fixture. By the early part of the next century, the ground soon became synonymous with rugby, and the Irish Rugby Football Union (IRFU) had its headquarters at the venue – the first stand was built in 1908.

During the 1980s, the Republic of Ireland soccer team under the auspices of the Football Association of Ireland (FAI) also made Lansdowne its home, and under the managerial expertise of Jack Charlton the team recorded some major results, including wins against Spain in 1989 to qualify for the FIFA World Cup in Italy the following year.

In 2007, the Lansdowne Road Stadium was demolished to make way for the new stadium – which took three years to complete at a cost of €410 million. To help with the construction costs of the new stadium, the IRFU and FAI sold the naming rights (a ten-year deal) to the Aviva Group Ireland.

The stadium reopened its doors in May 2010 with its seated capacity of 51,700, and boasts spectacular continuous curvilinear shaped stands enclosing on all four sides of the stadium.

Landmark fact: The Aviva Stadium hosted the prestigious 2011 Europa League soccer final between Portuguese teams Braga and Porto.

MUNSTER

Cork

Cork, or *Corcaigh* in Irish, means 'marshy place'. It was built on islands, surrounded by the River Lee, which were prone to episodes of flooding. Cork had its origins in the seventh century, when St Finbarr founded an abbey there and a settlement grew up around this monastic foundation. In 1172, after the Norman invasion of Ireland, Cork was surrendered to the English king and thirteen years later, it received its first charter. The city enjoyed a proud tenure as European Capital of Culture in 2005.

The National Monument

The National Monument on Grand Parade (one of the main thoroughfares that runs from South Mall to St Patrick's Street) in Cork was unveiled on St Patrick's Day 1906 by the famous Irish patriot Jeremiah O'Donovan Rossa, originally from Rosscarbery, County Cork. The monument commemorates the Irish nationalist rebellions of the United Irishmen in 1798, one led by Robert Emmet in 1803, the Young Irelander Rebellion in 1848 and the Fenian Rebellion of 1867. Architect D.J. Coakley designed the monument, while the sculptor was John Francis Davis.

Patrick Meade, the Mayor of Cork, laid the foundation stone on 2 October 1898. The spot chosen for the monument at the junction of the Grand Parade and South Mall had formerly been occupied by a statue of King George II.

Cork City Hall

The original Cork City Hall was destroyed during the early morning of 12 December 1920 by the Black and Tans (British Army) during the Irish War of Independence in an event known as the 'Burning of Cork'.

Following a design competition for a replacement building, designs by Alfred Jones and Stephen Kelly (Jones & Kelly Architects) were selected. The foundation stone of the new City Hall building was laid by Éamon de Valera on 9 July 1932, and it is one of the last classical stone buildings built on a grand scale in Ireland.

The cost of this new building was provided by the British Government in the 1930s, as a gesture of reconciliation. The City Hall, home to Cork City Council, was officially opened on 8 September 1936. A major extension to City Hall was opened in 2007.

Limerick

Luimneach, meaning 'bare spot', lies on the River Shannon, with the historic core of the city located on King's Island, which is bounded by the Shannon and the Abbey River. The city dates from AD 812, with a Viking establishment of a walled city, but it was the influence of the Normans that created key landmarks such as St John's Castle in 1200.

Thomond Park

Thomond Park is the home ground of Munster Rugby, one of the most successful and best supported rugby clubs in the world. Located on the outskirts of Limerick city centre and first opened to the public in 1940, it was completely redeveloped in 2008, allowing a capacity of 26,000.

One of the most famous occasions at Thomond Park was when Munster defeated the mighty New Zealand All Blacks by twelve points to nil on 31 October 1978.

The current form and design of the revamped stadium arose in 2006 after the Irish Rugby Football Union (IRFU) purchased the land adjacent to both sides of the pitch, which paved the way for larger stands. Work began in early 2007, and finished around eighteen months later in autumn 2008 with the erection of four unique stands.

On that reopening night in 2008, Munster again played the All Blacks. Two years later, Thomond Park witnessed another historic and memorable occasion when Munster played and triumphed over the touring international Australian team, adding yet another heroic landmark to the legendary reputation of this venue.

Landmark fact: In August 2013, Thomond Park was awarded the title of Best Rugby Stadium in the World, following a public vote by Rugby supporters across the world on the rugby blog Intheloose.com.

The Treaty Stone

The Treaty Stone is one of Limerick's most famous monuments. Limerick is sometimes known as the Treaty City, so called after the Treaty of Limerick that was signed on 3 October 1691 to end the Williamite War between William III of England (also known as 'William of Orange') and his father-in-law, King James II.

The Treaty Stone was traditionally regarded as the writing table on which the Treaty of Limerick was signed. According to tradition, the treaty was signed on a stone in the sight of both armies at the Clare end of Thomond Bridge.

CONNACHT

Galway

Gaillimh, which means 'stony river', lies on the River Corrib between Lough Corrib and Galway Bay. A fort was constructed in 1124 by the King of Connacht and eventually a settlement grew up around this fort. For centuries, Galway was dominated by fourteen families, known as the tribes of Galway, leading to it becoming known as 'the City of the Tribes'.

The mayor and the leading citizens usually came from these fourteen merchant families. Galway has had many famous visitors during its illustrious history, including Christopher Columbus.

Eyre Square/Kennedy Memorial Park

Eyre Square was officially presented to the city of Galway in 1710 by Mayor Edward Eyre. The area once simply known as 'the Green' was originally an assembly point in medieval times, popular for its proximity to the city gates, and to this day has remained the focal point of the city. The park is rectangular, surrounded on three sides by streets that form the major traffic routes into Galway city centre.

The park was officially renamed Kennedy Memorial Park after a visit by former US President John F. Kennedy, who made a speech in the square on 29 June 1963. Despite the renaming, the square is still widely known as Eyre Square. Kennedy was made a Freeman of Galway City and a bronze plaque near the fountain commemorates the event.

In 1984, a commemorative fountain was crafted, its shape emulating that of a Galway 'Hooker' sailing boat, and placed in the northern end of the square. It marked the 500th anniversary of the city's charter, granted by King Richard III in 1484, liberating Galway from the feudal lordship of the De Burgo clan.

Eyre Square underwent reconstruction works which were completed in 2006, costing the city €9 million. The new square layout contains 20 per cent more green space, new granite paving, 120 trees, and a children's play area.

The Spanish Arch

The Spanish Arch, which is located on the banks of the River Corrib in Galway, was built in 1584. It was originally an extension of the famous city walls, designed to protect the quays.

The Spanish Arch is so called because England and Spain were at war during the late sixteenth century, and in anticipation of a Spanish invasion this famous monument was built. Galway had become a fortified city in 1270, the 4.8-metre (16-foot) high walls protecting the 10 hectares (25 acres) of prosperous trading grounds and its inhabitants. Originally longer with four arches, it was formerly known as 'the Blind Arch' and it is located on the site more appropriately known as *Ceann na Bhaile* (the Head of the Wall).

The nearby Columbus sculpture was given to the city in 1992 from the city of Genoa, Columbus's birthplace. It marks the 500th anniversary of the discovery of America and commemorates Columbus's stay in Galway in 1477.

8

ABBEYS, CHURCHES AND SPIRITUAL LANDMARKS

Prior to the arrival of Christianity, places such as Newgrange were recognised as being vitally important. This Neolithic landmark was a place of spirituality, arguably as much as present-day cathedrals and churches are important places of worship.

Christianity spread to Ireland around the fifth century and at that time, the country was divided into a large number of small kingdoms. Most religious monasteries were founded in the sixth and seventh centuries and their founders came to be regarded as saints. This was Ireland's Golden Era, as it became a respected land of art and literature, culture and Christianity.

Ireland's patron saint, St Patrick, is as much an integral figure in Irish culture as he is in the country's Christianity. Indeed, Ireland has long been described as the Land of Saints and Scholars. In many respects centres such as Glendalough epitomise this notion, and St Patrick's arrival in AD 432 led to the mass building of churches.

The earliest Irish churches were of timber or other perishable materials. The stone church of Clonmacnoise was built by the High King Flann in 909, and is the oldest surviving dated stone church in the country. Since then, abbeys, churches and cathedrals have been built in all shapes and sizes. This chapter looks at a number of these notable landmarks, arranged on a province by province basis.

ULSTER

Dungiven Priory, County Derry
This priory is one of the oldest surviving churches in County Derry. Founded in 1100 by the O'Cahan clan – the local ruling family – the

priory belongs to the first wave of European monastic orders that arrived in Ireland to supplant the Celtic Church.

The church contains the tomb of Cooey na Gall O'Cahan, who died in 1385. The body is covered by a sword and beneath the effigy are small figures of armed warriors wearing kilts, who represent the O'Cahan chieftain's foreign mercenaries, from whom he derived his nickname, na Gall, or 'of the foreigners'. The church foundations were excavated in 1982, and shortly afterwards it was decided to put a roof on the chancel, in an attempt to protect O'Cahan's tomb from the elements.

Although the church has not been used since the eighteenth century, Dungiven Priory remains a religious site of sorts, as it is now an object of pilgrimage for people seeking cures for physical illnesses.

Grey Abbey, County Down

Grey Abbey is regarded as the best example of Anglo-Norman Cistercian architecture in Ulster. The abbey was founded in 1193 by Affreca, wife of John de Courcy, and Cistercian monks from Cumbria were based there.

By the late Middle Ages, the abbey had become decayed, and was dissolved in 1541, but in the early seventeenth century it was granted to Sir Hugh Montgomery and the nave was refurbished for parish worship which lasted until the late eighteenth century.

The abbey is an important historical site and is set in the beautiful landscaped parkland of eighteenth-century Rosemount House, consisting of the church with cloister and surrounding buildings to the south. It is based in the village of Greyabbey in north Down, named after the abbey.

Other sites linked with John de Courcy include Carrickfergus and Dundrum Castles (see Chapter 5).

Rathmullan Friary, County Donegal

This landmark was built by Ruaidhrí Mac Suibhne, the Gaelic chieftain of Fanad in north Donegal in memory of his eldest son who died in 1508. It has the distinction of being the last pre-Reformation Carmelite friary to be built in Ireland.

It consists of a nave-and-chancel church with south transept and some domestic buildings. At the end of the sixteenth century the friary was deserted by the Carmelite monks after a raid by George Bingham. The property passed to Bishop Andrew Knox in 1618, who fortified the friary and lived there. The Flight of the Earls – a key chapter in Irish history – took place from outside the priory in 1607.

Landmark fact: From the Rebellion of 1641 until 1988 the grounds were used for the burial of generations of Rathmullan people, together with many victims of naval warfare and shipwreck.

Saul Church and Down Cathedral, County Down

Two miles outside Downpatrick, this site is known as the Cradle of Christianity in Ireland. This church and round tower were built in 1932 in the Celtic Revival Style, of silver-grey granite, to commemorate the 1,500th anniversary of St Patrick's first church in Ireland. Close by, on the crest of Slieve Patrick is a huge statue of the saint. Bronze panels illustrate scenes from the life of Ireland's patron saint.

Tradition holds that St Patrick and his companions landed at the mouth of the Slaney River, a few miles from here, in AD 432. Patrick encountered Dichu, the local chieftain, who gave him a barn for shelter. The word for barn in Irish was *Sabhall*, from which 'Saul' is derived. It was here that he first preached, immediately converting Dichu. Legend has it that he died here on 17 March 461 and is buried in nearby Downpatrick.

For more than 300 years following Patrick's death there was an abbey on this site until it was plundered and burnt by Vikings. In the twelfth century Saul was re-founded as an Augustinian Priory, but it too was later plundered in the fourteenth century by Edward Bruce.

One wall of this abbey remains, along with an intact monastic cell in the old graveyard. The present church building, which replaced a very simple building that had been constructed in 1788, was erected to commemorate the 1500th anniversary of the landing of St Patrick and was opened on All Saints' Day 1933.

Downpatrick

Religious life in the town of Downpatrick has long been focused around the hill on its south-western border. Several orders of monks worshipped here from the sixth century onward, and a small congregation still gathers at the present-day Down Cathedral.

Cathedral Hill, where Down Cathedral stands, is far better known as the supposed burial ground of St Patrick, patron saint of Ireland. A well-worn tenth-century cross in the churchyard and a more recently placed granite slab inscribed with the saint's name mark his final resting place.

Landmark fact: Today prayer and worship continues at Saul, as it has done over the centuries. Services are held in the church every Sunday, and prayer is offered at different times throughout the week.

St Matthew's Church, Belfast

St Matthew's Church of Ireland Church was built in 1872 and is unique because of its trefoil shape and round tower. It is located in the Woodvale area of the city, and is sometimes referred to as The Shamrock Church. It is thought that St Matthew's is the oldest Christian site in Belfast, dating back to the first settlement in the area, around AD 455.

In 1855 a 'Bullaun Stone' was uncovered in the Shankill Graveyard, and it is believed this large stone dates back to Druid times, when it would have been used in a ceremony for pagan sacrifices. In early-Christian times, the stone was used as a baptismal font when the original church stood in the grounds, and is said to cure warts if the affected area is rubbed on the stone. It was removed to the grounds of St Matthew's Church in 1911. The church is now a Grade A listed building.

CONNACHT

St Nicholas's Collegiate Church, County Galway

The Collegiate Church of St Nicholas, located between Market Street and Church Street in Galway city is the largest medieval parish church in Ireland in continuous use as a place of worship. It is very much at the heart of Galway's life on the edge of the bustling Latin Quarter. The church is dedicated to St Nicholas of Myra, patron saint of children (he is sometimes referred to as Santa Claus) and of mariners – appropriate, given Galway's proximity to the Atlantic Ocean.

There is some disagreement about when St Nicholas's Church in Galway was built, but it is estimated to have been completed by 1320. At that stage, Galway was a fairly small new town. The inhabitants had great ambition, and built a huge church, bigger than many Irish cathedrals. The church was raised to the status of a collegiate church by letters under the seal of Donatus Ó Muireadhaigh, the Archbishop of Tuam, on 28 September 1484.

St Nicholas's Church has developed in various ways over the centuries, and a tour through the building reveals many interesting and entertaining monuments and memorials for the visitor. The baptismal font is estimated to be of late sixteenth-century or early seventeenth-century date, and is beautifully carved. Still used today, the dog carved into its side still keeps an eye on Galway's newest citizens as they are baptised.

Among the many visitors to St Nicholas's Church over the centuries, perhaps the most famous was Christopher Columbus, who prayed there during a visit to Galway from Italy in 1477. Legend has it that this was the last place that Columbus prayed with his crew before setting off to discover America.

Over the centuries, St Nicholas's Church has played a central role in the life of Galway city, and for many years the triennial elections of the mayor and corporation (city council) were held within its walls. It was used for Catholic Mass by the congregation of St Augustine's Church during the refurbishment of their church between April and December 2005. St Nicholas's Church of Ireland Church is regularly used also for worship by the Romanian and Russian Orthodox communities in Galway.

Landmark fact: The oldest tomb in the church is that of Adam Bures, known as the Crusader, whose grave marker dates from the thirteenth century.

Clonfert Cathedral, County Galway

Clonfert Cathedral, also known as St Brendan's Cathedral, is a twelfth-century structure on the site of St Brendan's sixth-century monastery in Clonfert. A monastery was originally founded on the site by St Brendan in AD 563. Known as 'the navigator' because of his legendary voyage across the Atlantic Ocean in the sixth century, he is buried in Clonfert.

The monastery was attacked several times by the Vikings, but was expanded and completed around 1164 in the Hiberno-Romanesque style. Characteristic decorations include abstract geometric patterns, and traditional Celtic designs. The Romanesque sandstone doorway is made up of six arches and richly carved with plants and animals. Inside, to the right of the altar, a carved mermaid represents Brendan's expeditions.

The west portal is considered one of the finest examples of twelfth-century carving in Ireland. Various educational and narrative values of the site, in combination with the interior design, make the cathedral equally valuable to Ireland's national history.

It was highly regarded in scholastic terms. It became an episcopal see, and in 1266 a bishop-elect was sent from Rome and conferred there. By the mid-sixteenth century, following the suppression of monasteries in Ireland by the English Crown, it was earmarked to become Ireland's first university by Queen Elizabeth to balance the Catholic influence of Clonmacnoise – but she opted for Dublin and the establishment of Trinity College (see Chapter 7).

Clonfert was restored as a Church of Ireland cathedral in 1664. The building today remains in use for worship as a parish church.

Boyle Abbey, County Roscommon

The Cistercian order of monks (sent by St Bernard of Clairvaux) founded Boyle Abbey in 1161 beside a small river that flows into Lough Key as a sister abbey for Mellifont in County Louth, their first abbey in Ireland, which they established twenty years earlier. The Mac Dermot family, who were the ruling lords of the area, funded the abbey building, and they were its patrons for two centuries.

In common with all Cistercian abbeys, Boyle consists of a group of structures that form a square, arranged around a central lawned area. The Cistercian buildings were not completed until around 1218 when the abbey was consecrated and named Boyle Abbey. Maurice O'Duffy was appointed by Mellifont Abbey as Boyle Abbey's first abbot.

There were various attacks on Boyle Abbey throughout its history. In 1202, the Anglo-Norman Lord William de Burgh ransacked the abbey. It was attacked again in 1235, and the Cromwellian army besieged it in the mid-seventeenth century.

Despite this, the ruins are impressive, dominated by a squat square tower that was added in the thirteenth century. Boyle Abbey is now a national monument under the care of the Office of Public Works and restoration work of this landmark continues.

> **Landmark fact:** Boyle Abbey was converted into a fortified castle by Cromwell's English forces in 1659.

Cong Abbey, County Mayo

Cong is surrounded by beautiful Connemara countryside on the Galway–Mayo border. Its Gaelic name, *Cunga Feichin*, meaning 'a narrow strip of land', is very informative and revealing, as it is situated on a narrow isthmus of cavernous limestone between Lough Mask and Lough Corrib. *Feichin* refers to the important role played by St Feichin, a French monk who arrived in Ireland and helped to found the Cong Monastery around AD 785. Sadly, this was destroyed by fire in 1100.

The majestic monastic remains that are the cornerstone of the historic village of Cong today are the relics of a monastery built by the High King of Ireland, Turlach O'Connor in 1123 for the Augustinian order of monks. This second version was a stone-built abbey complex surrounded by enclosed, well laid-out gardens, cobbled paths and stone bridges. The king also presented the monks with a gift – the Cross of Cong, one of Ireland's greatest treasures. It was kept in the abbey for centuries, and used daily by the abbot, who carried it at the head of the monks' processional prayer hour.

The Cross of Cong was acquired by the Royal Irish Academy in 1839. It is now kept in the National Museum in Dublin. The monastery continued as a site of worship and learning, until it was suppressed during the reign of King Henry VIII.

> **Landmark fact:** In 1951 John Ford's celebrated film *The Quiet Man* starring John Wayne, Maureen O'Hara and Barry Fitzgerald was made in the village of Cong.

LEINSTER

St Michan's Church, County Dublin

Just north of Arran Quay on Church Street in Dublin stands St Michan's Church, constructed in 1095 by the Vikings in honour of a saint whose origins are thought to be Danish or perhaps Welsh, and substantially rebuilt and completed in 1685. Indeed, it was the only church located on the north side of Dublin city until the following year.

St Michan's was renovated in 1825 and now functions as a parish church within the (Anglican) Church of Ireland. Inside is an eighteenth-century organ which the famous composer George Frederic Handel played his *Messiah* during a visit to Dublin, where it was first performed.

However, below the church are five long burial vaults that contain 'mummies' that attract many visitors to this quirky landmark. The crypt's combination of dry air and constant temperature, together with methane gas keeps corpses in a state of mummified preservation. Among the 'exhibits' are members of many of Dublin's most influential families from 1600 to 1800, as well as the Sheares brothers, John and Henry, who participated in the 1798 Rising.

Some of the others include a nun, a crusader (although historians dispute the accuracy of this) and a thief. The latter is identified as such because of a missing hand, amputated as penance for an earlier misdemeanour.

> **Landmark fact:** The death mask of United Irish leader Wolfe Tone is contained in one of the crypts under St Michan's Church.

Christ Church Cathedral, County Dublin

The earliest manuscript dates Christ Church Cathedral to its present location around 1030. Dúnán, the first Bishop of Dublin and Sitriuc, Norse King of Dublin, founded the original Viking church, which was probably subject to the Archbishop of Canterbury.

By 1152 it was incorporated into the Irish Church and within a decade the famous archbishop Laurence O'Toole had been appointed. This future patron saint of Dublin began a reform of the cathedral's constitution along European lines.

It was due largely to John Cumin, the first Anglo-Norman archbishop, that the Hiberno-Norse cathedral was replaced with a Romanesque and later Gothic cathedral, parts of which survive today.

In 1395, King Richard II sat in state in the cathedral to receive homage from the kings of the four Irish provinces, O'Neill of Ulster, McMurrough of Leinster, O'Brien of Munster and O'Connor of Connacht.

In the sixteenth century, reform again came from England when Henry VIII broke from Rome. He dissolved the Augustinian Priory of the Holy Trinity and established a reformed foundation of secular canons. In 1562, the nave roof vaulting collapsed, so the cathedral was in ruins and emergency rebuilding took place immediately. This temporary solution lasted until the 1870s.

In 1689 King James II attended Mass here and for a brief period, the rites of the pre-Reformation faith were restored. One year later, returning from the Battle of the Boyne on 6 July 1690, King William III gave thanks for his victory over King James II and presented a set of gold communion plates to the cathedral.

During the sixteenth and seventeenth centuries, Christ Church's crypt was used as a market, a meeting place for business, and at one stage even a pub, as a letter of 1633 shows that the vaults, from one end of the minster to the other, were made into tippling houses for beer, wine and tobacco.

The cathedral as it exists today (a two-year restoration of the cathedral roof and stonework was undertaken in 1982) is due to the extensive restorations and renovations carried out by the architect George Edmund Street (between 1871 and 1878) at the expense of a Dublin whiskey distiller, Henry Roe, who gave £230,000 to save the cathedral.

Mellifont and Monasterboice, County Louth

The historic ruins of Monasterboice are of an early-Christian settlement not far from the town of Drogheda in County Louth. It was founded in the late fifth century by St Buite, who died around 521. St Buite was an Irish monk and follower of St Patrick, and this was an important centre of religion and learning until the founding of nearby Mellifont Abbey in 1142.

The name Monasterboice is a part-anglicisation of the Irish name *Mainistir Buite*, meaning 'the Monastery of Buite'. The site houses two churches built in the fourteenth century or later and an earlier round tower, but it is most famous for its tenth-century high crosses. The round tower is about 28 metres tall (92 feet), and is in very good condition. The tower at Monasterboice was burned in 1097, destroying the monastic library and other treasures. However, it is still in excellent condition, though without its conical cap, and is the second tallest round tower in Ireland.

St Buite's monastery remained an important centre of spirituality and learning for many centuries. In 1142 the first Cistercians came to Ireland at the invitation of St Malachy, Archbishop of Armagh. He had visited the famous monastery of Clairvaux on a journey to Rome and, impressed by what he found there, asked St Bernard, the abbot, to train some of his companions in the monastic way of life.

These monks, together with some ten other French monks, became the founders of old Mellifont Abbey, about 3.2 kilometres (2 miles) from Monasterboice. The site was donated by O'Carroll, chieftain of Oriel. The monastery flourished and founded several other Cistercian houses in Ireland. Monastic life continued there until King Henry VIII's suppression of the monasteries in 1539.

Around 150 monks fled from Mellifont, and the buildings were handed over to Edward Moore, ancestor of the Earls of Drogheda who converted it into a fortified mansion. However, it went into gradual decline with attacks by Cromwellian forces and was used as William's headquarters during the Battle of the Boyne.

Mellifont Abbey was re-established in 1938 at Collon, County Louth by Archbishop, later Cardinal, Joseph MacRory, when he invited monks from County Waterford to found a new monastery on lands that had been part of the property of Mellifont Abbey.

Today the ruins of old Mellifont Abbey are in the care of Heritage Ireland.

Clonmacnoise, County Offaly

The early-Christian site of Clonmacnoise (*Cluain Mhic Nóis* in Irish, meaning 'Meadow of the Sons of Nós') is situated in County Offaly, located on the eastern bank of the River Shannon south of Athlone. It was founded by St Ciarán in AD 545 and in the early medieval period Clonmacnoise was at the crossroads of the two major routeways of Ireland – the mighty River Shannon and the Slí Mór (meaning the Great Way).

Clonmacnoise encompasses a cathedral, eight churches, two round towers, high crosses, grave slabs and a thirteenth-century ringfort. The early tenth-century Great Cross is over 3.65 metres (12 feet) high; while the South Cross dates from the ninth century.

The strategic location of the monastery helped it become a major centre of religion, learning, craftsmanship and trade by the ninth century and together with Clonard it was the most famous in Ireland, visited by scholars from all over Europe. It provided much of Ireland's finest Celtic art and illuminated manuscripts and the site supported a religious community that thrived throughout the Middle Ages.

Up until the last decade of the twelfth century Clonmacnoise had close associations with the Kings of Connacht. It was a burial place for the Kings of Connacht and Tara, including the last High King of Ireland, Rory O'Connor, who was buried here in 1198. The cathedral at Clonmacnoise was built in 904 by King Flann and rebuilt in the fourteenth century by Tomultach MacDermott.

The nearby O'Rourke's Tower is 18 metres (60 feet) high and was erected in 1134. On the outer boundary of the site are a number of churches, including Teampall Conor which was founded early in the eleventh century by Cathal O'Connor and used as a parish church from about 1790.

Largely protected by its isolation and surrounded by bog, Clonmacnoise could only be reached by boat and one road that ran along its boundary. However, in 1552 the English garrison at Athlone looted the monastery and left it beyond recovery.

Nowadays, the site stands as a preserved ruin under the management of the Office of Public Works. The graveyard surrounding the site continues to be in use and religious services are held regularly on the site in a modern chapel.

> **Landmark fact:** The site includes the largest collection of early-Christian graveslabs in Western Europe.

Glendalough, County Wicklow

As part of Wicklow Mountains National Park (see Chapter 4), Glendalough is particularly renowned for an early medieval monastic settlement founded in the sixth century by St Kevin.

Kevin, who was a hermit priest and a descendant of one of the ruling families in Leinster, studied as a boy under the care of three holy men: Eoghan, Lochan and Eanna. During some of his studies, he went to Glendalough. He was to return later, with a small group of monks to found a monastery.

St Kevin's monastic settlement was substantial, it was a 'city' with a round tower, several churches, a cathedral, farm, houses and a sizeable lay population, which enabled it to enjoy 500 years as one of Ireland's great ecclesiastical centres. Kevin's fame as a holy man spread and he attracted numerous followers.

The monastic site founded by St Kevin is pitched at the heart of the valley, helping to make it one of the most visited places in Ireland. There is a cathedral dating from the tenth to twelfth centuries and to the south of it is St Kevin's Cross, a massive slab of granite, carved in the eighth century. A local legend states that if one encircles the cross with one's arms and makes a wish concerned with healing, that wish will be fulfilled. There is also a round tower (see Chapter 5). But perhaps the most famous building on the site is St Kevin's Church (often called 'the kitchen').

Other important monuments in the vicinity include St Kevin's Cell and St Kevin's Bed. The cell was a small beehive hut built on a rocky spur over the lake and is said to be St Kevin's house.

Kevin died around 618, but for six centuries afterwards, Glendalough flourished. The *Book of Glendalough* was written there about 1131; and in the early decades of the next century, the dioceses of Glendalough and Dublin were united.

From that time onwards, however, the cultural and ecclesiastical status of Glendalough gradually diminished. Attacks by the Vikings in the ninth and tenth centuries and the destruction of the settlement by English forces in 1398 left it a ruin, but it continued as a place of pilgrimage.

The area is also associated with St Laurence O'Toole, Dublin's patron saint. He was born in 1128 and was a former abbot at

Glendalough and later Archbishop of Dublin. Laurence made a journey every Lenten season for a forty-day retreat in St Kevin's Bed.

> **Landmark fact:** Around AD 1042, oak timber from Glendalough was used to build the second longest 30-metre (98-foot) Viking longship ever recorded. A modern replica of that ship was built in 2004 and is currently located in Roskilde, Denmark.

Jerpoint Abbey, County Kilkenny

Jerpoint Abbey is one of the most complete Irish Cistercian monasteries. It is located close to the River Nore, near the medieval town of Thomastown. The abbey is believed to have been founded by a donation from the King of Ossory around 1160. It is still relatively intact and its fifteenth-century crossing tower dominates the surrounding landscape.

Jerpoint Abbey was established for a Cistercian sect of Catholic monks on the site of an earlier Benedictine monastery. The remaining ruins date from different time periods, but all of them are impressive in their ability to last. The tower dates from the fifteenth century, the church from the twelfth century and the transept chapels vary in age.

Among the notable carvings in the ruins are the saintly religious reliefs known as 'the weepers', and a sarcophagus that is surrounded by medieval Christian reliefs. Many of the pillars and incidental spaces in the ruined abbey are covered in similar figure carvings. Jerpoint Abbey is now under the care of the Office of Public Works.

MUNSTER

St Fin Barre's Cathedral, County Cork

One of Cork's most distinctive landmarks, St Fin Barre's Cathedral (Anglican), is situated in one of the oldest areas of the city, and forms a group with several other ancillary buildings. The name 'Cork' derives from the Irish *Corcach Mór Mumhan*, which means the 'Great marsh of Munster' and refers to the fact that the centre of Cork city is built on islands which are marshy and prone to episodes of flooding.

Legend has it that St Fin Barre was the son of Amergin, whose tribe was descended from Eochaidh Muidmheadoin, brother of the King of Munster. St Fin Barre eventually came to Cork in AD 606 where he founded a monastery with what became a renowned monastic school on the site of the present cathedral. Christian worship and learning has continued here ever since. St Fin Barre died in Cloyne in AD 623 and is said to have been buried in the graveyard somewhere near the east end of the present St Fin Barre's Cathedral.

In 1735 a 'new' cathedral was completed. This building retained the tower and spire of the old cathedral and was not highly regarded architecturally. It was demolished in the 1860s to make way for the present cathedral.

William Burges was appointed architect for a new cathedral in 1862, after a competition for which there were sixty-three entries. Burges drew up an overall iconographic scheme for the cathedral windows, and maintained control over all stages of the work. The cathedral is built of Cork limestone and the interior of Bath stone and the walls are lined with red Cork marble. Burges also designed stained glass, sculptures, mosaics, furniture and metal work for the interior.

Among the requirements of the competition was that the cost of the building should not exceed £15,000 and Burges was criticised by other architects because the cost of the towers, spires and carving was not included in his estimate. In the end some £100,000 was spent on the building. In 1865 the foundation stone was laid by Bishop John Gregg, although the towers and spires were not completed until 1879.

Ardfert Cathedral, County Kerry

This cathedral is located in the village of Ardfert in County Kerry, the location that St Brendan, a native of the area, founded a monastery in the sixth century.

There are three medieval churches, two Ogham stones and a number of early-Christian and medieval grave slabs on the site today. The earliest building is the cathedral, an early Gothic structure constructed primarily in the thirteenth century with large battlements added in the fifteenth century.

In the late sixteenth century Ardfert was caught up in the Desmond Rebellion and the cathedral was severely damaged, although it appears to have continued to function. During the Rebellion of 1641, the building was destroyed by fire and abandoned. In 1671, the south transept was rebuilt and served the Anglican congregation until the 1870s when a new Church of Ireland church was built in the village.

Scultpure of St Brendan the Navigator

Some 9.6 kilometres (6 miles) from Clonfert in the village of Fenit, a large bronze sculpture of St Brendan was erected in 2004 on Great Samphire Island, the rock around which Fenit harbour was built –

and close to the area where it is believed that Brendan was born around 484.

Gallerus Oratory, County Kerry

Located on the western tip of the Dingle Peninsula, this famous chapel landmark, *Gall Aras* ('shelter for foreigners'), is one of the most perfectly preserved of twenty such oratories in Ireland.

This early-Christian monument is estimated to have been built at some time between the seventh and twelfth centuries. It resembles an upturned boat, is constructed entirely out of locally sourced stone and is corbel vaulted. This entailed gradually overlapping the stones, so that each course projected slightly inwards until the arch was closed at the apex of the roof.

The church entrance is defined by a simple lintelled doorway located in the western wall. This was originally sealed by a wooden door that was secured in place by two stone brackets. A local tradition states that anyone who climbs through the tiny window is guaranteed access to heaven.

Rock of Cashel, County Tipperary

For more than a millennium, this formidable landmark has stood high above the town of Cashel in County Tipperary. The name originates from *Caiseal*, meaning 'stone fort'. The first mention of the Rock of Cashel was as a fortification of the Eoghanachta Kings of Munster in the fourth century.

It was allegedly visited by St Patrick during the following century, who converted Aenghus, the king of the time, to Christianity. This is why the famous Tipperary landmark is sometimes known as 'Cashel of the Kings' and 'St Patrick's Rock'.

This is also the place where St Patrick is supposed to have picked a shamrock in order to explain the doctrine of the Trinity – God the father, Christ the son and the Holy Ghost as three beings of the one stem.

According to local mythology the Rock of Cashel originated in the Devil's Bit, a mountain 32 kilometres (20 miles) north of Cashel, when St Patrick banished Satan from a cave, resulting in the rock flying through the air and landing in Cashel.

The Rock of Cashel was the traditional seat of the Kings of Munster for several hundred years prior to the Norman invasion. Few remnants of the early structures survive. The majority of buildings on the current site date from the twelfth and thirteenth centuries. The earliest and tallest of the buildings on the rock is the 27-metre

(90-foot) high round tower built in the early twelfth century. Its entrance was originally 3.65 metres (12 feet) from the ground.

But perhaps the most impressive part of the entire stronghold is Cormac's Chapel, considered to be one of the best examples of twelfth-century Romanesque architecture in Ireland. It was built between 1127–34 by Cormac McCarthy, who combined political and spiritual power as King of Desmond and Bishop of Cashel.

The cathedral was built in the century after Cormac's Chapel. It features a series of tall, high-set lancet windows. An interesting fact is that passages that ran through the nave and choir walls were supposedly for the outcasts of the community, so that they could watch the holy ceremonies without being seen themselves.

The Hall of the Vicars was built in the fifteenth century, and the ground floor contains the original St Patrick's Cross. Tradition suggests that the plinth was the coronation stone of the High Kings of Ireland, including Brian Boru who was killed during the Battle of Clontarf in 1014.

Landmark fact: After the Reformation, Queen Elizabeth appointed the Archbishops of Cashel, and perhaps the most notable of these was Miler MacGrath, who was previously the Roman Catholic Archbishop of Down and Conor. When Miler died at the age of 100, he was buried in the cathedral.

BIBLIOGRAPHY

BOOKS

Boylan, C.M., *The Little Book of Ireland* (The History Press, 2013)

Carey, Tim, *Croke Park: A History* (The Collins Press, 2013)

Clements, Paul, *Wandering Ireland's Wild Atlantic Way: From Bamba's Crown to World's End* (The Collins Press, 2016)

Cooper, Aiveen, *The River Shannon, A Journey down Ireland's Longest River* (The Collins Press, 2013)

Coyle, Cathal, *The Little Book of Donegal* (The History Press, 2016)

Coyle, Cathal, *The Little Book of Tyrone* (The History Press, 2014)

Dames, Michael, *Ireland: A Sacred Journey* (Element Books Limited, 2000)

De Breffny, Brian: *Ireland: A Cultural Encyclopedia* (Thames and Hudson, 1983)

De Breffny, Brian, (Ed.) *The Irish World* (Thames and Hudson, 1986)

De Buitléar, Éamon, *Irish Rivers* (Country House, 1985)

Dillon, Paddy, *The Mountains of Ireland* (Cicerone Press, 1992)

Eyres, Kevin and Kerrigan, Michael, *Ireland Landmarks, Landscapes & Hidden Treasures* (Flame Tree Publishing, 2015)

Fitzgerald, Mairéad, *Castles of Ireland* (O'Brien Press, 2007)

Flanagan, David and Creagh, Richard, *Exploring Ireland's Wild Atlantic Way* (Three Rock Books, 2016)

Flanagan, Deirdre and Flanagan, Laurence, *Irish Place Names* (Gill and Macmillan, 1994)

Gallagher, Clare, *Ireland: The Land of a Hundred Thousand Welcomes* (Summersdale Publishers, 2014)

Gerrard, David, *The Hidden Places of Ireland* (Travel Publishing Limited, 2007)

Gleeson, John, *The Book of Irish Lists and Trivia* (Gill and Macmillan, 1989)

Greenwood, Margaret, *The Rough Guide to Ireland* (Rough Guides, 1999)

Hamlin, Ann, *Historic Monuments of Northern Ireland* (The Universities Press, Belfast, 1987)

Harbison, Peter, *Guide to National and Historic Monuments of Ireland* (Gill and Macmillan, 1992)

Harris, Nathaniel, *Heritage of Ireland: A History of Ireland and its People* (Octopus Publishing Group, 1998)

Jackman, Neil, *Ireland's Ancient East: A Guide to its Ancient Treasures* (The Collins Press, 2016)

Lalor, Brian, *Ireland's Round Towers: Origins and Architecture Explained* (The Collins Press, 2016)

Levy, Pat and Sheehan, Sean, *Footprint Ireland* (Footprint Books, 2006)

Lucas, A., *Cattle in Ancient Ireland* (Boethius Press, 1989)

Lyle, Paul, *A Geological Excursion Guide to the Causeway Coast* (Environment & Heritage Service, 1996)

Manning, Conleth, *Early Irish Monasteries* (Country House, 2001)

McGuigan, Cathal, *The Little Book of Derry* (The History Press, 2015)

Meagher, Robert Emmett and Neave, Elizabeth Parker, *Ancient Ireland: An Explorer's Guide* (Arris Books, 2004)

Meehan, Carly, *The Traveller's Guide to Sacred Ireland* (Gothic Image Publications, 2002)

Nolan, Brendan, *Phoenix Park – A History and Guidebook* (The Liffey Press, 2012)

Nutan and Aston, Joe, *The Islands of Ireland* (Thames and Hudson, 2005)

Rankin, Peter, *Parliament Buildings, Stormont* (Ulster Architectural Heritage Society, 1999)

Simms, George Otto, *Exploring The Book of Kells* (O'Brien Press, 1988)

Stout, Matthew, *The Irish Ringfort* (Four Courts Press, 1997)

Wallace, Martin, *A Little History of Ireland* (Appletree Press, 1994)

Walsh, David, *Oileáin: A Guide to the Irish Islands* (Pesda Press, 2004)

WEBSITES CONSULTED

http://christchurchcathedral.ie/about/history/
http://corkcathedral.webs.com/early-foundation
http://discovertheshannon.com/listings/lough-ree/
http://iseegalway.blogspot.co.uk/p/landmarks.html

http://loughkey.ie/activities/park-and-estate/
http://riverbarrow.net/
http://whc.unesco.org/en/tentativelists/5528/
http://worldheritageireland.ie/bru-na-boinne/
www.antaisce.org
www.armagh.co.uk
www.askaboutireland.ie
www.athenryheritagecentre.com
www.atlasobscura.com
www.authenticireland.com
www.avivastadium.ie/stadium-info/history
www.bbc.co.uk/history/recent/troubles/overview_ni_article_07.shtml
www.blarneycastle.ie
www.bridgesofdublin.ie
www.britainirelandcastles.com
www.buildingsofireland.ie
www.castleleslie.com
www.cbl.ie
www.chrono.qub.ac.uk
www.corkpastandpresent.ie.
www.crokepark.ie
www.curiousireland.ie
www.destinationwestport.com
www.discoveringcork.ie
www.discoverireland.ie
www.discovernorthernireland.com
www.discovernorthernireland.com/loveheritageni/HistoricPlaces.aspx
www.dublincastle.ie
www.durseyisland.ie
www.giantcausewayofficialguide.com
www.glandorevillage.ie
www.greatlighthouses.com/lighthouses/rathlin-west-light/
www.guiness-storehouse.com
www.heritageireland.ie
www.heritageisland.com/attractions/kylemore-abbey/
www.hilloftara.org
www.irisharchaeology.ie
www.irishidentity.com
www.irishislands.info
www.kilmainhamgaolmuseum.ie
www.linenhall.com
www.lismorecastle.com
www.longfordtourism.ie

www.maps.ie/Irelands-islands.htm
www.megalithicireland.com
www.mellifontabbey.ie
www.mountainviews.ie
www.museumsofmayo.com
www.nationaltrust.co.uk
www.niassembly.gov.uk
www.npws.ie/national-parks
www.oireachtas.ie
www.rathcroghan.ie
www.roundtowers.org
www.saintsandstones.net/saints-killala-journey.htm
www.shannonheritage.com
www.ststephensgreenpark.ie
www.tcd.ie
www.theburrencentre.ie
www.theculturetrip.com
www.theirelandwalkingguide.com
www.thomondpark.ie
www.tipperary.com/swiss-cottage
www.titanicbelfast.com
www.treatystone.com
www.uisneach.ie
www.visitwicklow.ie
www.wmf.org

Visit our websites and discover thousands of other
History Press books.

www.thehistorypress.ie
www.thehistorypress.co.uk

The History Press Ireland